ON THE SANCTIFICATION OF PRIESTS

According to the Needs of Our Times

"You are the salt of the earth... and the light of the world" (Mt. 5:14-15).

Dissertated by

REV. FR. REGINALD GARRIGOU-LAGRANGE, O. P.
Master of Sacred Theology and Member of the Academy of Saint Thomas

Translated by Reverend Paul M. Kimball

Dolorosa Press
Camillus, New York

2013

Copyright © 2013 Paul M. Kimball
ISBN: 978-0-9883723-9-9

Copy Editor: Mrs. Patti Petersen (petersenpatricia59@gmail.com)

To order additional copies, please contact:

Dolorosa Press
www.dolorosapress.com

Reverend Father Garrigou-Lagrange's title "Sacrae Theologiae Magister" (S.T.M.) or "Master of Sacred Theology" is the name given to an honorary title bestowed by the Roman Catholic Order of Preachers (Dominicans) on its most distinguished scholars. Thus it is a "master's degree" in the most ancient sense and thus can be likened to an honorary doctorate conferred only upon Dominicans who are already scholars of theology. The recipient must be a full-time professor for ten years and have published books and articles of international scholarly repute. The initial nomination is made by the friar's own province (local distrinct) and then must be approved by the intellectual commission of the Generalate in Rome. The final decision is then made, after review, by the Master of this Order and his council.

We have examined the book of Father Reginald Garrigou-Lagrange, O. P., Master in Sacred Theology: *On the Sanctification of Priests According to the Needs of Modern Times*, and we deem that it truly conforms with the doctrine of Saint Thomas, and that it would be useful for it to be published.

Rome, Angelicum   July 1, 1945

FRAY MICHAEL BROWNE, O. P., *Master of Sacred Theology*
FRAY ROS. GAGNEBET, O. P., *Doctor of Sacred Theology*

Imprimi potest
Rome, Sancta Sabina   March 12, 1946

FRAY M. ST. GILLET, O. P., *Master General*

Nihil obstat quominus imprimatur
Casali, April 6, 1941

Can. Theol. ALOYSIUS BAIANO, *Rev. Eccl.*

Imprimatur.

Can. ODDONE, *Vicar General*

Explanation of the Abbreviations Used in Citations

The *Summa Theologiae* of St Thomas Aquinas is cited by part (I, I-II, II-II, III), question, and article. For example, ST II-II, q. 23, a. 3, ad 1 means, the second part (half) of the second part, question twenty-three, article three, reply to the first objection. "Obj." refers to an objection within an article.

The *Enchiridion Symbolorum* (Denzinger, H. and A. Schönmetzer, eds.) has been herein abbreviated as Denz. This is a classic collection, albeit partial, of Church documents in Latin arranged historically.

TO THE HOLY MOTHER OF GOD

MOTHER OF ALL MEN

UNIVERSAL MEDIATRIX

AND QUEEN OF PEACE

AS A SIGN OF HIS GRATEFUL HEART

AND FILIAL OBEDIENCE

THE AUTHOR

READILY DEDICATES THIS WORK

INTRODUCTION

I. — Concerning the necessity of a more profound faith.

This subject needs to be discussed at the beginning on account of the dangers that arise from the very serious errors that have now spread throughout the world, and on account of the insufficiency of the remedies to which we often have recourse.

These most pernicious errors, which are now scattered throughout the world, tend towards the complete dechristianization of nations. This began with the **revival of paganism** in the sixteenth century, which is the revival of pagan pride and sensuality among Christians. This decline progressed with **Protestantism**, through its denial of the sacrifice of the Mass; of the power of sacramental absolution, hence Confession; through its denial of the infallibility of the Church, and Tradition or Magisterium; and denial of the necessity of observing the precepts for salvation. These are the four very great denials that overthrow the foundations of Christian life. Next, the **French Revolution** openly strove for the dechristianization of society, according to the principles of **Deism and Naturalism**; more precisely, the idea that God, if He exists, does not care about individual persons but only about universal laws. Hence, sin is not an offense against God, but is only an act against reason, which itself evolves perpetually; thus theft was considered to be a sin as long as the right of private property was admitted; but if private property, as the Communists say, is something which belongs to the community, then it is private property itself which is the theft.

The spirit of the revolution, on the other hand, led to **Liberalism**, that tried to keep a middle attitude between the doctrine of the Church and the modern errors. But Liberalism concluded nothing; it was not affirming nor was it denying, but always distinguishing, and always prolonging discussions, because it had not been able to solve the questions that were arising from the abandonment of the principles of Christianity. Hence, Liberalism did not suffice to handle the matter, and so after it there came **Radicalism**, more opposed to the principles of the Church, under the name of "Anticlericalism," not to mention Antichristianism. Such are the Masons. And now Radicalism led to **Socialism** and Socialism to **Materialistic Communism and Atheism**, as is now in Russia; and it sought to invade Spain and other nations by denying religion, private property, the family and country; as well as by reducing the whole of human life to an economic life, as if only the body existed, and as if religion, the sciences, the arts, and law were the inventions of those who wished to oppress others and possess all private property.

Against all these denials of Materialistic Communism, only the true Christianity, or Catholicism, can effectively resist, because it alone contains the Truth without error.

Hence, **Nationalism** cannot efficaciously resist Communism. Nor, in the religious order, can **Protestantism**, as it is in Germany and in England, resist Communism, because it contains grave errors, and error kills the societies which are based upon it, just as a serious sickness destroys an organism. Protestantism, like consumption or cancer, is a deadly malady on account of its rejection of the Mass, Confession, the infallibility of the Church, and the necessity of observing the Commandments.

Now what follows from the aforesaid errors in regard to the *legislation of nations*? This legislation slowly becomes *atheistic*. It not only withdraws from the existence of God and from the divine (revealed) law, both positive and natural, but it contains many laws opposed to the divine (revealed) law, e.g. the *law of divorce* and the *laws concerning neutral schools*, becoming ultimately atheistic, according to the three levels: primary schools, academies or high schools, and universities. Religion is often reduced to a more or less rationalistic history of religions in which Christianity is viewed only in a Modernistic way, as now having attained a higher stage of evolution of the religious sense which is always being altered, such that there can be no immutable dogmas nor immutable precepts. Finally there comes every kind of *liberty* of cults or religions, and *impiety* or *irreligion* itself. Now the repercussions of these laws on the whole of society are immeasurable, e.g. concerning the law of divorce, in any year thousands of divorces in whatever nation destroy families and leave the children to be without education and without direction, who thus become either incompetent, proud, or even the worst children. Likewise, from atheistic schools every year go forth many men or citizens who possess no religious principles. And therefore, instead of them possessing faith, hope and charity, they possess a disoriented mind, concupiscence of the flesh, concupiscence of the eyes, the desire for money, and the pride of life. All these things are set forth in its own naturalistic system under the name of *secularized* or *freethinking* ethics without obligations or sanctions, in which there sometimes remains some vestige of the Decalogue, but a vestige which is always changeable.

If, however, the most lamentable effects of these pernicious errors do not yet clearly appear in the first generation, they are manifested in the third, fourth, and fifth generations according to the law of acceleration in descent. It is as in the acceleration of falling bodies: if in the first second the velocity of descent were to be twenty, in the fifth second it would be a hundred. And this is the direct opposite of the progress of charity, which according to the parable of the sower is sometimes thirtyfold for one, fiftyfold for another, and a hundredfold for yet another.

This is a true dechristianization or apostasy of nations. This matter is correctly expounded in a long letter of the great Spanish Catholic, *Donoso Cortes,* written to Cardinal Fornari in order to be presented to Pius IX; its title is: *Concerning the generative principle of today's more serious errors* (thirty pages) and *Discourse of the actual state of Europe* (1850). See the *Works* of this author in five volumes, Madrid, 1856. Further, the same group of errors is exposed in the Syllabus of Pius IX, 1864, (Denz. 1701).

The origin of these errors is: *God, if He exists, does not care about individual persons,* but only about universal laws. Hence, sin is not an offense against God, but is only contrary to our reason, which always evolves. From this follows that there was no original sin, nor consequently the redemptive Incarnation, nor regenerating grace, nor sacraments, which are for causing grace, nor a sacrifice, nor therefore is the priesthood useful, nor is prayer something useful.

However, Deism does not seem to be true, because if men individually do not need God, why should it even be admitted that God exists in heaven? Rather it ought to be admitted that *God comes into being in humanity*, and this is the same tendency to progress and to the happiness of all men concerning which Socialism and Communism speak.

What is, therefore, according to these principles, the *means to discern what is true from what is false*? That unique means is *free discussion*, whether in parliament or in another way, and this freedom is absolute, such that nothing is exempt from being summoned before its tribunal, whether it be the subject of the utility of divorce, the utility of private property, the utility of the family or the utility of religion for the people.

And so the discussion remains most free, as if there were no divine Revelation, e.g. it is said that divorce is prohibited in the Gospel, but this matters little.

From all these things arise, it is clear, great disturbances, innumerable miscarriages of justice, crimes; and no remedy is found except of always increasing the manpower of the civil governor or of those enforcing civil discipline: (the police) and the army.

But the force of civil government (the police) serves those who have authority; and, not rarely, after them come their enemies, who command the opposite thing. And from a new policy, private property having been taken away, patriotism is generally taken away, which is, as it were, the soul of the army.

Whence these remedies do not suffice to keep order and to prevent serious and perpetual disturbances, because it is no longer admitted that there exists a divine law, not even a natural law inscribed by God in our hearts. (And all these are proofs *per absurdum* of the existence of God.)

Consequently it must be concluded, with Donoso Cortes, that *these societies* which are founded upon false principles or atheistic legislation, *tend to death*. In them individual persons can still be saved, by the help of grace, but these societies as societies tend to death, *because error,* in which they are founded, *kills;* just as consumption or cancer progressively and infallibly destroys an organism. — Only the Christian and Catholic faith can resist these errors and again Christianize society, but to this end is required a condition: *a more profound faith*, according to that passage, "This is the victory which overcometh the world, our faith" (1 Jn. 5:4).

* * *

On the insufficiency of the remedies to which we often have recourse.

Two remedies are indeed employed which are in themselves excellent, namely, on one hand the *apostolate* of Catholic Action, and on the other hand *the study of the doctrine of faith and morals*; but often is lacking the pinnacle of study which the ancients called *contemplation*, which ought to be the *fountainhead of the apostolate* or which ought to fructify in the apostolate as St. Thomas says: "From the fullness of contemplation is derived teaching and preaching" (II-II, q. 188, a.6). This was true in the Apostles after Pentecost, in St. Peter, in St. Paul, in St. John, in the apostolic Fathers, in St. John Chrysostom, in St. Augustine, in St. Gregory, in St. Anselm, in St. Bernard, in St. Dominic, in St. John of the Cross, in St. Ignatius, in St. Francis Xavier, in St. Vincent de Paul, in St. Francis de Sales, in St. John Bosco, in St. Joseph Cottolengo, in the Curé of Ars and in J. Baptist Manzella. In other words, there is often lacking in priests an interior life intense enough that it be the soul of the apostolate.

Catholic Action has indeed already produced many fruits in Europe and America for the restoration of Christian life among workers, among farmers and among university students; these very good fruits are observed in Italy, France, Switzerland, Spain, Holland, and Belgium; in Canada, Mexico, Argentina, etc. Nevertheless, not infrequently the priests who direct Catholic Action are too much absorbed in "bureaucracy": in the external organization of the works and in its propaganda, and so their interior life is lessened, and therefore they cannot nourish the interior life of others. With difficulty is sufficient time found for reciting the breviary even very hurriedly; further, excessive familiarity of the younger priests with youths of both sexes not infrequently lessens their dignity and influence. Finally, the more educated *laity* often become speakers, quasi-preachers (conference speakers), and from this arise the two deviations of religious sentimentalism and humanitarianism, because he who speaks or quasi-preaches, often does not live enough from a profound faith, nor from apostolic charity. If the preacher or speaker does not live enough by God, he speaks, for example, according to democratic aspirations. He indeed says what is to be discussed about Christian democracy, but one must be attentively vigilant that it be, and remain, truly Catholic. In other respects, as not rarely happens, not a supernatural but a natural inclination prevails, which does not ascend, but rather descends, according to the law of the least effort (law of the least resistance).

The Masons use this deviation, so that in the Church the apostolate declines to practical naturalism, which is at least a practical denial of the supernatural life. — Whence in the apostolate there is often lacking the interior life of the priest, which ought to be the very soul of the apostolate. (See Dom. Chautard, *The Soul of the Apostolate*.)

* * *

Another very good remedy is applied, namely, the *study of the doctrine of faith and morals*, and in these latter times, philosophical, exegetical, sociological and also ascetical and mystical study has been strengthened, and often it is made in a more scientific manner than previously. It is indeed very well distinguished from a pious exhortation that would be without solid doctrine.

But the *distinction* ought not to be a *separation*; and, not rarely, study is unhappily separated from the interior life, such that it is not inspired by it, nor does it tend directly enough to fostering it. The interior life is neglected, and thereupon study is made in an exclusively natural manner, without the spirit of faith, and hence the interior life is more and more diminished. Even in ascetical and mystical theology, theses concerning spirituality are expounded, but these disciplines do not tend directly enough toward the sanctification itself of priests, and hence they do not produce significant fruit. It would be better to live from prayer than to write a treatise about prayer. Many undeservedly say about religious books, "Either they are scientific books or they are books of vulgarization"; but higher books such as the Gospel, the Epistles, and books of the great spiritual authors, are neither scientific, that is to say, technical, nor of vulgarization, but of contemplation.

For this reason the remedies brought forth, although they are very good in themselves, are applied in a very imperfect manner and produce little fruit.

Thus we do not rise up again to higher things, and we realize this, but to escape sadness we hurry back to a superficial optimism, either from our temperament or from our choice, and this inferior optimism does not bring a remedy that can stop the lessening of the interior life.

Thus not only does it not bring a remedy, but an interior peace is sought after as well, which is not the peace of God and joy from God, but rather it is a joy concerning oneself without foundation, and it is sometimes silliness and folly.

Conclusion: From all these things it follows that the interior life is absolutely necessary for the priest and apostle that he may arrive *at a profound* and irradiating *faith* to be communicated to the faithful, that they might resist the very pernicious modern errors which are a deadly poison. And so we return to the definition of apostolic life given by St. Thomas: "To contemplate divine things and to transmit the things contemplated to others" (II-II, q.188, a.6); and where he says, "As it is better to enlighten than merely to shine; so it is better to transmit things contemplated to others than only to contemplate... (And this manner of living) is very near to the perfection of bishops, who are the successors of the Apostles." He says (*Ibid*) that the preaching of the divine word ought to proceed from the fullness of contemplation or of the interior life.

It follows from this that the *sanctification of the priest* is of the highest importance, and much more necessary than "the full natural development of our personality"; this last expression is naturalistic, and can be used by an unbeliever or an atheist. It originates from forgetfulness of the first petition of the Lord's Prayer, "Hallowed be thy name," through which we seek God's glory, or that God's name be kept holy by men (II-II, q.83, a.9).

There follows also the great necessity of the *very good celebration of the Mass* by adjoining to Christ's renewed unbloody sacrifice, the personal daily sacrifice, with a spirit of *mortification and reparation*; while the world seeks after an agreeable life (modern comfort).

There follows the necessity of *intimate prayer*, without which the spirit of prayer cannot be possessed, such that the liturgy sometimes is lowered to the level of religious aestheticism. Of old, St. Bernard knew this very well. When presiding at the Divine Office in choir, he saw above one religious his guardian angel, who was writing the psalmody in golden letters; above another his angel was writing it in silver letters; above the third religious the angel was writing with ink; above the fourth he was writing with water without color; above the fifth religious his angel was writing nothing and he was holding his hand and wing extended, to show that this religious was in no way praying, and possessed no spirit of prayer.

There equally follows the necessity of a serious *examination of conscience*, while on the contrary, in some seminaries, it is asked of the preacher of the exercises that he not speak specifically about the examination of conscience, but rather about *introspection*; and others have spoken about psychoanalysis. This is a very open digression from the supernatural spirit toward practical naturalism; for the examination of conscience ought to proceed from infused prudence and from faith enlightened by the gifts of the Holy Ghost, while introspection is something natural derived from psychology, and in like manner is psychoanalysis, concerning which Freud speaks in the sense of materialism and sensualism. This change of vocabulary shows and reveals the thoughts of hearts and the spirit of practical naturalism in place of the true supernatural life.

If, however, these true and more elevated remedies are neglected, the priest possesses only a superficial faith, which touches only the outer surface of Sacred Scripture, and not a truly profound and irradiating faith. The priest perhaps speaks of the necessity of *dynamism in the apostolate*, but this dynamism is seen to be particularly natural and differs from the apostolic spirit of St. Peter on the day of Pentecost, of St. Paul, of St. John Chrysostom, of St. Augustine, of St. Bernard, of St. Dominic, of the Curé of Ars and St. John Bosco.

This matter is very well noted by Pius XI in his Encyclical *On the Priesthood* dated December 20, 1935, where he treats of the virtues of the priest, and specifically concerning his piety.

For it does not suffice, as is clear, that a priest possess a high intelligence, great learning, and be gifted with eloquence; even with all these things his life can remain sterile, as seen with Lamennais and Loisy. Because then the priest perhaps does not seek God nor the salvation of souls, but instead he seeks himself, his natural satisfaction in intellectual labor and in an unsanctified natural activity, which does not come forth from the interior life of faith, hope, charity and prayer, and therefore does not produce supernatural effects, namely, the salvation of souls.

On the contrary, the priest who has little natural intelligence, but a great supernatural faith, a true interior life and a sincere piety, exercises a very fruitful apostolate.

This apostolate is modest in its exterior form, but bears much fruit and saves very many souls, not by speaking about dynamism. In the moment of his death this priest will be judged according to the level of his own love of God and of souls and according to the forgetfulness of himself, or abnegation.

And now by following this true and traditional way of priestly formation *faith becomes profound* even without the help of high theological speculation or knowledge of the Eastern languages; this faith, already firm and living daily, becomes more deep, because it is intensively increased with charity, it is enlightened by the gifts of wisdom, understanding, knowledge, counsel, and piety, and hence is *diffusive* of itself, and so it touches hearts and converts sinners. It is made apparent as a higher sense, namely, as the *Christian sense,* which surpasses common sense just as infused faith enlightened by the gifts surpasses natural reason.

The saintly Parish Priest of Ars possessed this Christian sense in the highest degree (see *The Ecclesiastical Retreat* of Fr. Cormier: St. Vincent de Paul, St. Philip Neri, St. Francis de Sales, etc.).

Confirmation: If the prayer of the priest through the recitation of the Office, the celebration of Mass, and pious meditation does not arrive at the true spirit of prayer and to a certain contemplation of divine things, which is the soul of the apostolate; if he does not attain to this normal summit, he deteriorates and departs into a *mechanical custom* (routine), and the recitation of the breviary seems to be the motion of a machine for grinding grain (a prayer mill).

* * *

Let us return now to the exposition of the question, namely, to the present spread of serious errors that are a poison of souls, especially materialism and atheistic Communism. These errors have very great influence through the atheistic legislation of many nations, in which there is the law of divorce; absolute indifferentism which is taught in primary, secondary, and higher schools; together with all manner of liberty of worship even to the point of absolute liberty of religion and impiety. These effects, as we have stated, do not yet appear after the first generation, formed thus, but after the fifth and sixth generation the effects are terrible. In any one year thousands and thousands of divorces occur, which destroy entire families and leave the children without guidance, so that many of these children become truly evil and sometimes the very worst. Likewise, the school which is said to be neutral, but is in reality atheistic, forms in any one year thousands and thousands of unbelievers, or citizens who have no religious principles, but in place of Christian faith, hope and charity in them there prevails "the concupiscence of the flesh, the concupiscence of the eyes and the pride of life," under the appearance of a secularized ethic without obligation and sanction, which is always evolving. In time past, theft was condemned because the right of private property was admitted, now many men, namely the Socialists and Communists, say, "Private property itself is theft," by which someone claims for himself that which ought to be owned by everyone.

These errors, written in modern legislations, lead nations to death as a cancer in an organism kills that organism. This becomes apparent not after the first generation, but after the fifth or sixth. And the Masons use all these things for the destruction of Christianity, and for the dechristianization of nations.

There is therefore *an urgent need of a moral resurrection*, a need to rise up to higher things: *sursum corda*. This need is expressed in the divine precepts, especially in the greatest precept of the love of God and neighbor.

What, therefore, is to be concluded in practice? It is necessary to say with St. Augustine, that which was cited by the Council of Trent, "For God does not command impossibilities, but by commanding admonishes you both to do what you can do, and to pray for what you cannot do, and assists you that you may be able" (Denz. 804).

It must be concluded therefore that *new graces are always offered to souls*, particularly to priestly souls, in this important critical time, that they may arrive at the loftiness of their obligations in the present circumstances.

Indeed many are inclined to think that God also prepares great graces for priests that they may attain to the aforesaid faith, not only firm and living, but also profound, penetrating, savoring, and irradiating, which they ought to communicate to the Christian people that they might be able to resist the modern errors, which are a deadly poison, and that they might again find the pure and truly breathable air of the Christian ages. Thus would be verified the words in I Jn. 5:5: "This is the victory which overcomes the world, our faith."

So as to conclude, it should be noted: By means of the *union of theological study and the interior life*, the deviation is avoided which is the *confusion* of both together. Study and the interior life ought to indeed be *distinguished* without confusion, but they ought not to be *separated*, and they ought to be *united*. Otherwise theological science, from being confounded with piety, would lose its objectivity and immutability, and on the other hand the interior life might possibly be reduced to the theses pertaining to spirituality. Thus sacred theology would unhappily be reduced to the intellectual expression of subjective religious experience, in somewhat the same way as is found among the Modernists; and on the other hand, the interior life would become too intellectual, it would become a theory of the interior life, and it would lose its realism, its profound interconnection and fruitfulness.

These two things ought *not to be separated*, but *distinguished* and *united* as was the case in St. Augustine and St. Thomas and all the doctors of the Church.

Thus are distinguished and united the body and the soul, the head and the heart, blood and water; in this way also the Church and State, likewise the diverse classes of society, and moreover, in the family, the parents and children.

If a distinction becomes a separation in our organism death follows, so likewise in society and also in our life which ought to be both intellectual and spiritual. This grace of the union of study with piety is implored through the intercession of the Doctors of the Church, who are never declared Doctors by reason of their learning before they are canonized for their sanctity. (Concerning this union of study and piety, see the life of St. Alphonsus by Fr. Berthe. There are in that place two excellent chapters of great importance).

II. — Concerning the supernatural and infallible certitude of infused faith with respect to the interior life.

State of the question: Although all theologians admit that Christian faith, notwithstanding its obscurity, to be most firmly certain, nevertheless not all explain this certitude in the same way. There are especially two opinions proposed in many centuries. The first does not hold that the faithful infallibly know through infused faith itself the formal motive of faith; the second affirms and defends this as the apple of the eye.

The first opinion is defended by the Nominalists: by Durando, Gabriel Biel, by Scotus, by Molina, Ripalda, Lugo,

Franzelin, Billot, Bainvel, van Noort, and Harent; it holds that the faithful *naturally* know the formal motive of faith, namely, the authority of God revealing and the very fact of revelation; from this, that we naturally know God, we can neither be deceived nor deceive; and likewise the fact of revelation can be naturally known from its supernatural proofs, especially from miracles.

Criticism: A difficulty immediately appears against this opinion. It is indeed true that the certitude of infused faith is materially and extrinsically based upon the rational knowledge of the proofs of revelation, but it is formally and intrinsically based upon something higher, otherwise the greater certitude would be lowered to a lesser certitude. Moreover, rare are the faithful who have seen miracles with their own eyes and who were able to examine them sufficiently enough to judge with certainty concerning their supernatural origin. Therefore the faithful do not generally have more than a *moral certitude* concerning the proofs of Christian Revelation, by means of human testimonies often not known in a discriminating way.

Thus, as say many other theologians, if the certitude of Christian faith were ultimately founded upon this moral certitude of the fact of revelation confirmed by various proofs, this certitude of the faith would not be very firm and infallible *except hypothetically*, that is to say, by it being supposed that from elsewhere it be certain that God has revealed the Trinity, the redemptive Incarnation, and the Church's infallibility for the proposing of these mysteries; it is supposed, of course, that the preaching of these mysteries does not proceed out of a *natural* evolution of the religious sense in the subconscious of the prophets and of Christ, as the Modernists have said, which borders upon the faith being dissolved into a heap of probabilities.

The second opinion is defended by the Thomists and also in some way by Suarez, and it maintains that the faithful, through infused faith itself, *infallibly and supernaturally* know the formal motive of faith as *that by which and that which is believed,*[1] not by a discursive, but a most simple and a most firm adherence, which immensely surpasses the quite inferior, morally certain

---

1 *quo et quod creditur.*

conclusion of apologetics, namely, the conclusion concerning the evident credibility of the mysteries of the faith or concerning the fact of revelation confirmed by certain proofs.

I have cited many texts of St. Thomas and of both old and recent Thomists in the book *de Revelatione*, vol. I, chap. 14, pp. 464-497.

This opinion is proved by a three-fold argument:

Firstly, it is proved by reason of the absolute infallibility of the faith; secondly, by reason of the essential supernatural motive of the faith; and thirdly, by reason of the supernaturality of the faith itself.

Firstly, it is proved **by reason of the absolute infallibility of the faith.** For the fact of revelation is not only proposed with a moral certitude from history relating Christ's preaching and miracles, but also it is infallibly proposed by the Church, which defines this revelation to have been properly supernatural, and that it did not naturally come forth from the subconscious of the prophets. But that which is thus infallibly handed down by the Church is to be supernaturally believed by all. Therefore the faithful ought to *supernaturally* believe Revelation, together with the revealed mysteries; as St. Thomas says: "We with one and the same act believe God (revealing) and in God (revealed)" (II-II q.2, a. 2). And the infused virtue of faith so perfects the intellect, says St. Thomas, "that the intellect should infallibly tend to its object."

Otherwise, if the formal motive of faith is only naturally known, by means of human testimony, the certitude of faith would only be *hypothetically* infallible, and not absolutely. And then the words of St. Paul would not be infallibly verified: "When you had received of us the word of the hearing of God, you received it not as the word of men, but *as it is indeed, the word of God,* who worketh in you that have believed" (I Thess. 2:13).

The second argument is taken **from the essential supernatural motive of faith.** And indeed that which is essentially supernatural, by it being formally such, cannot be naturally known, because the true and being are convertible, for the true and being are intelligibly known. But the formal motive of infused faith is essentially supernatural, for it is the authority of God revealing essentially supernatural mysteries. The supernaturality of this formal motive transcends the supernaturality of a naturally knowable miracle. He who reveals is God, not as the Author and Ruler of nature, but as the Author of grace and our Father in heaven; whence Christ says, "I confess to thee, O Father, because thou hast hid these things from the wise and prudent, and hast revealed them to little ones" (Matt. 11:25). He also says, "Blessed art thou, Simon Bar-Jona: because flesh and blood hath not revealed it to thee, but my Father who is in heaven" (Matt. 16:17).

The formal motive of infused faith is inaccessible without grace, as are the formal motives of infused hope and charity. Otherwise these infused virtues would not be necessary. (Cf. St. Thomas II-II, q.6, a.1.)

The third argument is taken **from the essential supernaturality of the faith itself.** For faith according to Revelation is a gift of God (Eph. 2:8), it is "the substance of things to be hoped for" (Heb. 11:1), and it is a supernatural virtue (Vatican I, Denz. 1789). — But a habit and an act are specified by both the formal object *quo* and *quod* of the same order. — Therefore the formal object *quo,* or formal motive, by which per se infused faith is specified, is of the same order and hence cannot be attained without it (faith). If it could be attained without it, infused faith would not be absolutely necessary for believing as one must for salvation, but it would only be necessary for believing more easily and more firmly, as the Pelagians said. Likewise, infused hope and infused charity would not be necessary except for hoping and loving more easily, and in the same way neither would the state of grace be necessary.

So by one and the same act of faith, as St. Thomas says, we believe God (revealing) and in God (revealed) (II-II, q.2, a.2; ibid. q.4, a.8). Thus faith is more certain than any natural knowledge, and its infallible certitude greatly surpasses the moral certitude to which those who fruitfully read books of apologetics generally arrive.

Fr. Lacordaire, in his seventeenth *Conference on Our Lady,* very well shows the supernaturality and infallibility of the faith:

"Take a scholar who studies Catholic doctrine, who is constantly saying, 'You are blessed to have the Faith; I would also like to have it, but I cannot.' And what he says is true: he cannot yet have it... But once this scholar gets on his knees: he feels his misery as a man, raises his hands to heaven, and says, 'From the depths of my misery, my God, I cry to Thee!' And at that moment, something happens within him; scales fall from his eyes, a mystery is accomplished — and behold he is changed! He is a man who is meek and humble of heart: he can die for he has converted to the truth. (A mystery is accomplished means that the infused light of the Faith had been given to him). A warm understanding thus accomplishes between two men what logic would not have done in many years. And such is the way that a genius is sometimes enlightened. A convert will tell you: 'I have read, I have reasoned, I have wanted, but I just could not; and one day without knowing how, was it on a street corner or near my fireplace, I was no longer the same, I believed... and what took place in me at the moment of this definitive conversion is of an absolutely different nature than that which preceded it... remember the two disciples who were going to Emmaus.'"

Therefore, infused faith is, as it were, a superior spiritual sense, and, as it were, an infused musical sense, by which the heavenly harmony of divine revelation is heard. — So truly "faith is the substance of things to be hoped for, the evidence of things that appear not." In this passage it is evident that its most firm certitude excludes every deliberate doubt, notwithstanding its obscurity, and it greatly surpasses the moral certitude which generally arises from the study of apologetics.

From this follows that the loss of infused faith is a great misfortune, but faith is not lost except through a mortal sin which is directly against faith itself, nor would a sin against the external confession of the faith suffice, as was Peter's sin during the Lord's Passion.

Therefore this faith remains most firm even in the state of mortal sin, but then it is called *unformed* or *dead*, and *non-living* or not vivified by charity; the works, for example the works of mercy, which proceed from it in this state of death are called dead works. But when it is informed by charity it is called living faith, and when it is perfected by the inspiration of the gifts of wisdom, understanding, and knowledge, it is called faith enlightened by the gifts, or penetrating or savoring, which is identified with the contemplation of divine things.

This teaching is confirmed from the passive purification of the spirit, in which appears the loftiness of the formal motives of faith, hope and charity, insofar as these motives immensely surpass all the secondary motives that exist, e.g. the harmony of the supernatural mysteries both with the natural truths and with our aspirations. This harmony is no longer apparent at this time, it is hidden in darkness, and the three motives of the theological virtues show themselves as three stars of the first magnitude in the night of the spirit; it would not help much at this time to read a good book of apologetics, but one must pray to obtain the actual grace necessary for the most firm and very meritorious adherence to the faith amidst the vehement temptations of this passive purification. In the end the soul finds an immutable refuge in the authority of God revealing.

These considerations suffice with regard to the supernaturality and infallibility of infused faith. Now one must speak about the spirit of faith or about the supernatural spirit.

III. — Concerning the spirit of faith and concerning the supernatural spirit and also concerning its origin

The spirit of faith is the inclination to consider and judge all things under the light of faith, in a supernatural manner. And this is necessary for Christian living, just as to judge according to right reason is necessary to living reasonably and not merely sensibly.

St. Paul gives most beautiful examples of the spirit of faith, when he says: "By faith Abraham offered Isaac; he offered his only begotten son, who had received the promises...accounting that God is able to raise up even from the dead...By faith Moses left Egypt, not fearing the fierceness of the king Pharao; for he endured as seeing (God) that is invisible...By faith, the Israelites passed through the Red Sea as by dry land: which the Egyptians attempting, were swallowed up. —By faith the prophets conquered kingdoms, wrought justice, obtained promises, stopped the mouths of lions (as Daniel did), quenched the violence of fire... Others were stoned, they were cut asunder, they were tempted, they were put to death by the sword; of whom the world was not worthy" (Hebrews 11). All these died in the faith yet they had not seen the promised Christ. What therefore ought we to do, who have come after Christ? "Let us run by patience to the fight proposed to us: looking on Jesus, the author and finisher of faith, who having joy set before him, endured the cross, despising the shame, and now sitteth on the right hand of the throne of God" (Heb. 12:1-2).

But to live in the spirit of the faith one ought to view all things under its light, namely God, ourselves, our neighbor and daily events, such that all things are viewed as it were "with the eye of God" (St. Thomas).

Firstly, **God Himself is to be viewed with the spirit of faith**, otherwise He is known badly and erroneously, namely, by means of our inordinate passions and prejudices, as opposed to the testimony which God gives of Himself. Then, during prayer, the soul hears itself and not God. So when it has sensible consolation, it thinks that it is truly making progress; and when it is in sensible aridity, it thinks itself to be going backwards, it is depressed and doubts of God's love for itself; it forms to itself a false judgment about God.

If, on the contrary, God is viewed with the spirit of faith, He does not appear to us by means of our inordinate passions, but *in the mirror of the mysteries of Christ's life and death*; in the victory of Christ crucified over the devil, sin, and death; in the influence of the Blessed Virgin Mary; in the wonderful life of the Church, and the communion of Saints, or in the life of the Church militant, suffering, and triumphant.

For this, however, it is required that the eye of faith be freed from the veil of self-love, by which the contemplation of divine things is impeded; with this veil nothing appears except the shadows and difficulties of the mysteries. From this is shown the necessity of the internal mortification of one's own internal judgment and one's own will, more precisely of the will not conformed to the divine will, from which arises great obscurity in the mind. For everyone judges according to his own inclination. Through this progressive purification there appears more and more the loftiness of God, His goodness, the most tender mercy of Christ, the beauty of the Church and of the religious life.

Secondly, **we ought to view ourselves in the light of faith.** If we view ourselves in the light of natural reason alone, we see nothing but our natural qualities, which we exaggerate and amplify, and then, seeing our limits, we fall into depression, or pusillanimity. This fluctuation is frequent.

We rarely consider in our soul *the treasure of the life of grace,* of the infused virtues, of the gifts of the Holy Ghost, of the Most Holy Trinity dwelling in us, of the fruit of Eucharistic Communion, and of the greatness of our vocation, in which all the actual graces for attaining to perfection are virtually offered to us. It should be petitioned that, already on earth, we might see what our sacerdotal vocation entails, as we will see this immediately after death in the moment of our particular judgment.

If we view our soul in the light of faith, little by little we also know our *predominant fault,* lack of a supernatural spirit and the levity of mind, the vanity according to which we judge and speak in a merely human way. Thus would appear what comes from God in our souls and what from our deficiency, that is, the white and black.

Thirdly, **we also ought to view our neighbor in the light of faith.** Often we see him only with the light of natural reason obscured by our prejudices, pride, ambition and envy. Therefore we approve in our neighbor that which pleases us, that which is useful to us and that which he owes to us; and we reprove that which troubles or inconveniences us, and sometimes that by reason of which our neighbor surpasses us, and then we fall into detraction or into rash judgment inspired by self-love.

On the contrary, if our neighbor is viewed in the light of faith then what proceeds from God appears in him, that is to say, in superiors there consequently appears the authority of God, whom one must obey without criticism and discussion, both with the whole heart and promptly. Likewise, in persons who are not naturally pleasing to us are seen *souls redeemed by Christ*, who perhaps are closer to the heart of Christ than we ourselves. Then our supernatural gaze penetrates the covering of flesh and blood which impedes the vision of souls. And then is shown that two immortal souls never meet each other by chance, and at least one ought to bring about the welfare of the other (by giving good example). We ought to merit this so that we may see souls as good and holy, especially those with whom we live and whom we often ignore.

But in persons who naturally please us, if they are viewed in the light of faith, their supernatural virtues appear which elevate our affection, and also certain defects appear, which perhaps we can expose to them with benevolence so that they may attain to greater perfection.

Finally, **daily events are to be viewed in the light of faith**, all events whether happy or unhappy. For every event can be considered in three ways: Firstly, only in its *sensible* aspect; secondly, in its *rational* aspect, as it would be examined by a philosopher or an unbelieving historian; thirdly, in its *supernatural* aspect, by reason of which these events concur for the glory of God and for the salvation of souls, or is not opposed to these ends.

In this way also are to be viewed wars, conflicts between men of the same nation, and the very divisions between Catholics, in order that they might not become greater. But to see this supernatural or providential aspect of events, a Christian ought to live by God and be not detained by lesser things. Indeed in order that a man be freed from excessive love of lesser things, it is sometimes good that he be deprived of them, that he be stripped of them. And so St. Thomas says, "That we see the stars it requires that the sun does not shine any longer." Thus a Christian king who loses his kingdom, such as Louis XVI in France before his death, sees better the *kingdom of God*, than he had seen on his throne.

Through this spirit of faith, the saints arrived at a *contempt of themselves*, and to loving humiliations, in order that they might become more perfectly conformed to Christ humiliated for our salvation, despised and crucified. So, as says Augustine, the love of God built the city of God in which the saints love God unto the contempt of themselves; and disordered love of self built the other city, in which evil men love themselves unto the hatred of God.

He who lives thus in the spirit of faith would certainly arrive at a profound, penetrating, practical faith, diffusive of itself, for resisting today's errors. Then would be verified the words in I Jn. 5:4: "This is the victory which overcometh the world, our faith."

IV. Concerning the supernatural signs of this spirit and how in practice we ought to live by it [2]

This spirit is a manner of considering, judging, loving, willing and acting; it appears on every page of the Gospel, e.g. Matt. 13:46, where it is told about the merchant seeking good pearls: "Who, when he had *found one pearl of great price, went his way*, and sold all that he had, and bought it." This precious pearl is a figure of the supernatural spirit. Likewise (*ibid.* v. 44) where it is said: "The kingdom of heaven is like unto *a treasure hidden in a field*; which a man having found, and for joy thereof goeth, and selleth all that he hath and buyeth that field." — Again, when St. Paul says: "Mind the things that are above, not the things that are upon the earth," (Col. 3:2) this supernatural spirit is actually the spirit of faith, confidence in God, as well as love of God and our neighbor. But the signs of it are its fruits, "For by the fruit the tree is known" (Matt. 12:33), namely, humility, abnegation, piety and the three theological virtues (Encyclical of Pius XI *On the Priesthood*). The supernatural man is called by St. Paul "the new man": "And be renewed in the spirit of your mind and put on the new man, who according to God is created in justice and holiness of truth" (Eph. 4:23).

---

2 This is taken from the above cited *Spiritual Exercises* of Venerable Fr. Cormier, O. P.

The principle signs are the following, from the manner of conducting oneself with respect to the sources of sanctification.

The first sign is a *taste for Sacred Scripture*, inasmuch as it contains the Word of God, God's letter for saving men, so to speak, with its very beautiful variety taken from its simple narration, e.g. from the book of Tobias, to the high dogmatic heights of the four Gospels and the Epistles of St. Paul. The language of Sacred Scripture thus is, as it were, the *maternal language* of the Christian, because it is the Word of God, our adoptive Father. And now if the Christian truly tastes the words of Sacred Scripture, human eloquence, even the greatest, pleases less and less, because it does not contain the word of salvation, or the words of eternal life. One sentence alone of Sacred Scripture nourishes, enlightens, and in adversity strengthens the soul. Sacred Scripture is something much higher than a simple exposition of dogma divided into specialized treatises, for it is a sort of ocean of revelation, and in it is found a foretaste of eternal beatitude.

The second sign of the supernatural spirit is the *veneration of religious authority*. The natural man often does not see anything in the authority of his Superior except hard requirements of public order, which without this authority would not be able to stand. The natural man does not see in his dependence upon a superior something salutary; and therefore he limits this dependence as much as is possible, as does the state with respect to the Church, as if the authority of the Church were not something in itself something excellent even for the present life.

On the contrary, the Christian who has the supernatural spirit views this matter more from on high. He acknowledges with veneration *a certain emanation of the divine authority* in the authority of his Superiors, and for him to obey them is profit and glory. He not only obeys the regulations of the Superiors, but also their wishes and counsels. And he finds in this dependency a certain special joy for his soul. Thus he is raised above himself, saying, "To serve God is to reign." Hence St. Paul says: "Now therefore you are no more strangers and foreigners; but you are fellow citizens with the saints, and the domestics of God, built upon the foundation of the apostles and prophets, Jesus Christ himself being the corner stone" (Eph. 2:19). This is a glorious obedience which brings with it great security.

The third sign is the *desire for the sacraments*, "as the hart panteth after the fountains of water." The supernatural man sees in the sacraments not only religious ceremonies, but also fountains of grace by which Christ's merits of infinite value are applied to us. He not only believes in their efficacy, but he also has experience of this as well. Thus he runs to these sacred fountains promptly and eagerly; and hence weekly Confession and Holy Communion always produce in him ever more sweet fruits. He understands very well that each and every communion ought to be substantially more fervent and more fruitful than the preceding communion, because each one not only preserves but also augments charity and thus normally disposes one to a better communion on the following day, although the sensible devotion, which is accidental, can become less.

The supernatural man not only has a quasi-intellectual love with respect to Jesus Christ really present in the Eucharist, which is sometimes a complacency in our own thought or in the idealistic abstraction which we form in our mind; but from the Real Presence there also results for him a *real society*, a stable and intimate union with Jesus Christ. Thence all the acts of the day receive something from this vivifying presence. It is a life with God and the life of God Himself and Christ in us.

The sacramentals also, such as holy water, then produce a beneficial impression as water that is living and cold in the heat for the thirsty traveler. Equally the indulgences for the supernatural man are a precious gift, because he has a vivid idea of the gravity of sin, of the rigor of divine justice, of the infinite value of Christ's merits and also of the value of the merits of the Blessed Virgin Mary and the saints. Thus man may be renewed from day to day.

The fourth sign is *esteem for liturgical prayer*, inasmuch as we ever more see in it the great prayer of the Church, as a quasi-song of the spouse of Christ accompanying the sacrifice of the Mass, which is the unbloody continuation of Christ's sacrifice and prayer. Thus is understood that liturgical prayer has a special power to obtain the efficacious graces that we need. Participation in this public prayer is actually a grace, just like a diffused light in which our mind is placed for an hour. It is better to recite the Office in choir before the most Blessed Sacrament than individually outside of choir. Accordingly, the Divine Office's fruitfulness and variety appears more and more, but also its greater simplicity, which is above the fleeting time as a prelude of eternity. The Office thus celebrated greatly disposes to *secret mental prayer*, which is *another sign* of the supernatural spirit. Of old, in the thirteenth century, there was not a prescribed hour for mental prayer in the religious Orders, but the monks and nuns spontaneously, without obligation, after Matins and Lauds, made time for mental prayer, unto which liturgical vocal prayer performed with the spirit of faith disposes. But when religious did not any longer make mental prayer spontaneously, then an hour was prescribed to perform it, and then it was often less intimate and living, but rather mechanical sometimes, reduced to discursive meditation in some book, in the beginning of the day before any other exercise; and thus gradually the term "meditation" has become prevalent, and the term "mental prayer" has remained in use more so in the contemplative Orders.[3]

The fifth sign is *an inclination to mortification.* This propensity is indeed aware that our nature has been brought forth from God, that in it are precious faculties ordered to the true and the good. However, it does not forget that our nature is fallen, as is seen by the concupiscence of the flesh and of the eyes, and the pride of life, from which arise the seven capital sins, and from them other graver sins. Everyone judges according to his own inclination, which needs to be rectified. Christian grace as such, which configures us to Christ who suffered for our sins, inclines to this. It inclines to (making) a holocaust.[4] Whence, the

---

3 Dom. Pourrat seems to ignore this in his work, *The Christian Spirituality*; he seems to think that before the sixteenth century, when mental prayer was not being regulated, the religious were not applying themselves to it. On the contrary they were making it spontaneously without obligation, and better, in a manner more contemplative, at the end of the psalmody, because good psalmody disposes to a more intimate and personal mental prayer.

4 See St. Thomas in III, q. 62, a. 2.

renewed man always considers that "the flesh lusts against the spirit" as St. Paul says (Gal. 5:17). Therefore, the supernatural spirit causes a holy hatred against whatever is inordinate and dissolute in us; and hence, this is shown in the spirit of sacrifice, which destroys whatever is inordinate in us and consequently gives peace or the tranquility of order. Nothing better gives peace than the spirit of sacrifice.

The sixth sign of the supernatural spirit is *forgetfulness of oneself* or *of one's own personality*. It is indeed true that many saints who were initiators of great works and founders of religious Orders confidently used the faculties which they had received from God, as St. Paul, St. John Chrysostom, St. Augustine, St. Dominic, St. Thomas, St. Ignatius, St. Francis Xavier, etc., but in reading their lives, we see that they were *diffident about themselves* and that they were always fighting against self-love and the subtle pride within themselves. In this as in their other virtues they greatly surpass us. The saints, by denying themselves, understood practically that full progress of our personality consists in the fact that we are able to say: "I live, no longer I, but Christ lives in me"; this is as if to lose one's own personality, that the personality of Christ might be substituted for it. So they arrived to a certain *superior impersonality*, which overcomes all of one's own judgment and all self-will, so that nothing remains in them except the judgment of God and the will of God, just as in somewhat the same way in Christ there is not a human personality, but only the Word's divine personality. That which is ontologically verified in Christ is somewhat morally verified in the saints. The perfect do not live to themselves but to God, not for themselves but only for God and for souls, in the perfect and holy forgetfulness of themselves. This is the clearest sign of great charity and hence of the supernatural spirit of the renewed man, because "they have put off the old man...who is corrupted according to the desire of error" (Eph. 4:22). Thus the words of St. Paul are verified in the saints, "Our old man is crucified..., that the body of sin may be destroyed, to the end that we may serve sin no longer" (Rom. 6:6). —These are therefore the principle signs of the supernatural spirit in the man renewed by the grace of Christ.

* * *

To finish this chapter, it needs to be said practically *how we ought to live according to this supernatural spirit* in either ordinary and foreseen circumstances, or in unforeseen circumstances and in indeterminate affairs or of free choice. Now it is clearly evident to everyone that holy things are to be treated in a holy manner, e.g. to celebrate Mass or assist at it, and that one must resist temptations which manifestly draw (one) to evil.

But between these two extremes, between holy things are to be treated in a holy manner and a manifest evil is to be avoided, there is a *middle region* of indeterminate affairs, which remain *of free choice (ad libitum)*; in other words, which are left to our choice. And in these matters men are divided by the choice which manifests their hearts. Venerable Fr. Cormier notes, for example: Some call beauty that which is worldliness; moderation that which is a weakness to be avoided; honor that which is pride; or prudence that which is opportunism or utilitarianism inspired by egoism; indeed sometimes they call conscience that which is a deformation of a Christian conscience, e.g. when something very good is asked of them they reply, "In conscience I cannot"; thus they call "conscience" that which is a manner of life preferred by them in that it is agreeable and avoids inconveniences. — Fr. Cormier, in his Spiritual Exercises, gives this example, "If certain persons who are generally motivated by the spirit of piety, humility, and mortification, apparently or really go out of their way a little, there sometimes arises a rebellion as if there were an intolerable abuse, an inadmissible disorder, provocation and a forbidden injury."

On the contrary in matters left *to free choice* others immediately recall to mind the words of St. Paul, "Mind the things that are above, not the things that are on earth." The saints spoke thus, and they often acted above common prudence, under the inspiration of the Holy Ghost, without which they did nothing great. Especially Christ greatly surpassed common prudence, and when He first announced His Passion, Peter said to Him, "Lord, be it far from thee, this shall not be unto thee," and Jesus responded to him, "thou art a scandal unto me because thou savourest not the things that are of God, but the things that are of men" (Matt. 16:23).

In unforeseen matters, in which there is no time for reflection for choosing a convenient manner of handling oneself, *nature shows itself to be what it is*, with its egoism;[5] but even on these occasions the supernatural spirit of certain men will appear, e.g. in an unforeseen danger a generous man immediately runs to the aid of the afflicted. The friends of God quickly recognize each other, even if they were to come from distant lands and do not speak the same language.

What ought to be practically concluded regarding the supernatural spirit, especially for the priest?

One must labor with energy to obtain this spirit. To this end one ought to consider not indeed the little good that has been accomplished, but that which remains to be accomplished, according to that saying of Paul, "Stretching forth myself to those that are before" (Phil. 3:13). Excessive congratulations should not be made for the good already accomplished, and we ought to especially call to mind the good yet to be accomplished.

We also ought to say to ourselves, "For to me, to live is Christ, and to die is gain" (Phil. 1:21). For some men, says St. Thomas, their life is hunting, for others it is military exercises, for others their life is intellectual study, but for a Christian his life is Christ, because Christ is the object of his faith, of his thoughts, desires, and of both his affective and effective love. His conversation is with Christ. One ought to say to Him: "Impress, O Lord, a living love towards Thyself in my heart."[6]

Blessed is the supernaturally restored man, who, "being rooted and founded in charity" so far as he has renounced himself

---

5 *Il naturale ritorna al galoppo in un movimento primo-primo, sed etiam longius.*

"Chase away the natural and it comes back at a gallop in an instantaneously reflexive (*primo-primi*) movement, but also for a longer time."

6 The final cause impresses a love towards itself in the agent.

and created things, depends on God alone; thus he does not find pleasure except in divine things. Consequently, nothing impedes the kingdom of God in him and he is gradually assimilated to Christ; hence his ministry, notwithstanding its difficulties, in the end is always fruitful. For after he has labored, studied, written, and preached, the Holy Ghost gives fruitfulness; even if this priest were, naturally speaking, of mediocre ability, it suffices that one have great faith.

What a great joy it is when a priest at the end of his life will have arrived at this! And truly we can do this, because "God does not command impossible things, but by commanding He admonishes us to do what we can and to ask from Him that which we cannot do." Indeed God certainly calls us to sanctity, because He calls us to heaven where there is no one but saints. Now if this is indeed true for any Christian, all the more for the priest who participates in Christ's priesthood.

Authors consulted

Commentaries of St. Augustine and St. Thomas on John 10, 17, on the Epistle to the Hebrews, on Tim. and Titus. - St. John Chrysost., *On the Priesthood.* - St. Ephrem, *On the Priesthood.* - St. Gregory, Dialogue 4, 64. - St. Greg. Nazianz., *Prayer II.* - St. Paulinus of Nola, *Epist. XI to Sever.* - St. Cyprian, *Epist.* 77. - St. Bernard, *De. Consideratione.* - St. Peter Damian, *Opusc.* 18. - St. Albert the Great, *On the Sacrifice of the Mass; Mariale.* - St. Bonaventure, *On the Three Ways.* - St. Thomas, *On the Perfection of the Spiritual Life;* II-II, q. 184-185, and the Commentary of Passerinus *On the States of Men - Imitation of Christ*, book 4. - Cardinal Bona, *On the Sacrifice of the Mass* (ascetical work). - Bossuet, *Explanation of the Doctrine of the Church on the Mass.* - Ch. de Condren, *The Idea of the Priesthood and the Sacrifice of our Lord Jesus Christ.* - J. J. Olier, *Treatise on Holy Orders; The Interior Life of the Blessed Virgin Mary.* - St. Louis Grignion de Montfort, *Treatise on the True Devotion to Mary.* - Ven. Chevrier, *The True Disciple.* - St. Peter Julian Eymard, *The Most Holy Eucharist; Meditations for Spiritual Exercises for Priests*, 4 corsi, Torino 1934. - Cardinal Mercier, *The Interior Life, Call to Priestly Souls*, 1919 Brussels. - Silv. Maria Giraud, Missionary of La Salette: *Priest and Victim.* - I. Grimal, Mariste, *The Priesthood and the Sacrifice of Our Lord Jesus Christ*, Paris 1926; *With Jesus, Forming in Us His Priest*, Lyon, Vitte 1925. - J. Perinelle, O. P., *The Priesthood*, Editions du Cerf 1936. - Rev. Fr. H. M. Cormier, O. P., *The Three Ways of the Spiritual Journey*, Rome 1899, 3 vol.

CHAPTER I

ON THE OBLIGATION OF TENDING TO PERFECTION

In this chapter there are four distinct questions:

Firstly, whether *all Christians* ought to tend to perfection (cf. St. Thomas, II-II, q. 184, a. 3);

Secondly, that concerning the special obligation of tending to perfection for *religious*, by reason of a vow, and concerning the state of perfection;

Thirdly, whether *the clergy* ought to tend to perfection by reason of their ordination and duties (whether priests are in a state of perfection);

Fourthly, what sort of perfection is required for *a bishop*? (the perfection to be exercised) (II Tim. I, 3-14; Pontifical; St. Thomas, II-II, q. 184, a. 4, Commentary of Passerini; Suarez, *On the State of Perfection*, book I, chap. 15 and 16).

Article 1.

Whether all Christians ought to tend to perfection?

State and difficulty of the question: It is not a question about the lowest perfection which excludes only mortal sins, nor that of a middle perfection which excludes fully deliberate mortal and venial sins, but about perfection properly so-called which excludes deliberate imperfections and a remiss manner of acting. Here is not treated merely the invitation to perfection properly so-called, of which there is no doubt; all men are invited to perfection properly so-called.

The question is concerning the existence of a general *obligation* for all Christians of tending to the perfection of charity. Nevertheless, it is not here treated concerning the special obligation whose violation would be a special sin, as in the religious state, but concerning the general obligation.

The difficulty arises when we try to reconcile certain statements of the Lord Jesus Christ which at first glance seem to be opposed to each other.

On the one hand Christ says to the rich young man, "*If thou wilt be perfect*, go, sell what thou hast, and give to the poor... and come follow me" (Matt. 19:21). These words, "If thou wilt be perfect," seem to express a counsel, and not an obligation. Therefore not all Christians are held to tend to perfection. This does not seem to be obligatory except for those who have already promised to follow the evangelical counsels. Regarding this difficulty, cf. II-II, q. 184, a. 3, ad 1.

On the other hand, however, Christ said to all men, "*Be you therefore perfect*, as also your heavenly Father is perfect" (Matt. 5:48), and in his Commentary on Matthew's Gospel upon this saying of the Lord, St. Thomas says, "The clergy more than the laity are held to the perfection of an outstanding life; but all are held to the perfection of charity," namely, they are held to tend towards it.

Moreover, in the *Summa Theologica* (II-II, q. 184, a.3), St. Thomas proves that perfection essentially consists not in the counsels but in the precepts, for the first precept is without measure, namely: "Thou shalt love the Lord thy God with thy whole heart, and with thy whole soul, and with all thy strength, and with all thy mind" (Lk. 10:27). And therefore according to St. Thomas, perfect charity falls under the precept as an end to be attained.

St. Augustine, St. Thomas and St. Francis de Sales held that all men ought to tend to the perfection of charity, everyone according to his own condition. And so the perfection of charity falls under the precept as an end.

How are these words of the Lord to be reconciled: "If thou wilt be perfect..." and, "Be thou perfect"?

To this question thus posited, a true response according to the mind of St. Thomas seems to be rightly expounded by Cajetan and by Passerini commenting upon II-II, q. 184, a. 3; by Fr. Barthier in his book *On Christian Perfection and on Religious Perfection;* and by Fr. A Weiss, O. P., *Apologia of Christianity*, vol. 5, index:

Perfection. I have expounded this question at length in: *Christian Perfection and Contemplation,* vol. 1, pp.215-244; and *The Three Ages of the Interior Life,* vol. 1, p. 267 ff.

Answer: This answer is contained in four propositions:

1. All Christians are strictly obliged to appreciatively love God above all things.

2. All ought to tend to the perfection of charity, by the force of the supreme precept, but each one according to his own condition, this man in the state of matrimony, this man as a lay brother, and this man as a priest in the world.

3. No one, nevertheless, is held to actually have an uncommon charity or the charity of the perfect.

4. Nor are all held to directly and explicitly tend to it through the fulfillment of the counsels.

First proposition: *All Christians are strictly obliged to love God above all things*; this is the Lord's commandment: "Thou shalt love the Lord thy God with thy whole heart, and with thy whole soul, and with thy whole mind. This is the greatest and first commandment... And thou shalt love thy neighbor as thyself" (Matt. 22:37-39). Likewise, Deut. 6:5; Lk. 10:27; Mk. 12:30.

Whence, everyone is held to love God *at least appreciatively or in estimation* (love of esteem), if not intensively, above all things, and more than themselves. And as St. Thomas says: "One escapes (or avoids) transgressing the precept, *in whatever measure* one attains to the perfection of divine love. The lowest degree of divine love is to love *nothing more than God*, or *contrary to God*, or *equally with God*, and whoever fails from this degree of perfection nowise fulfills the precept" (II-II, q. 184, a.3 ad 2).

As Fr. Barthier (1, 218) observes, from this precept the modern liberties are condemned: liberty of worship, every kind of liberty of writing, of teaching, etc., which bestow the same rights to truth and error, good and evil – as if God, the supreme Truth and Highest Good, did not have a most strict and imprescriptible right to the obedience of our intellect and will, to be loved above all things. Whence, to acknowledge and to defend these liberties without limit and subordination to God is to turn oneself away from God, and to act against God. Indeed to be neutral in practice between liberalism and Catholicism is to love something equally to God. The love of God, even in its lowest degree, ought to have dominion over all our affections, such that truly, according to the rule of St. Thomas, "nothing is loved more than Him, or contrary to Him, or equally with Him: and whoever fails from this degree of perfection nowise fulfills the precept."

Now someone *appreciatively* loves God above all things when he wills to avoid every mortal sin. Thus a good Christian mother although she more intensively loves her own son whom she sees and touches, nevertheless she appreciatively loves God more than her own son.

Second proposition: *All Christians are held to tend to the perfection of charity, each one according to his own condition* (Barthier, vol. 1, pp. 419 and 315; cf. Passerini, *On the States of Men*, p. 758, n. 13; in II-II, q. 184, a. 3).

This proposition seems exaggerated to many Christians, who falsely reckon that only priests and religious are held to progress in charity. This is a very widespread error. Others admit the aforesaid proposition theoretically as being true, but they do not perceive its whole fruitfulness in practice.

Let us see: firstly, the foundation of this proposition in Scripture, and secondly, how it is proved theologically.

1. Now this proposition is equivalently expressed in many passages of *S. Scripture* e.g.: "Be you perfect as your heavenly Father" (Matt. 5:48); "He that is just, let him be justified still" (Apoc. 22:11). Likewise in diverse passages in the New Testament which are collected in Concordances under the word "grow": "grow in grace, and in the knowledge of God" (II Pet. 3:18); "Laying aside all malice... that thereby you may grow unto salvation" (II Pet 2:2); "But doing the truth in charity, we may grow up in him who is the head (of the Church), even Christ" (Eph. 4:15); "Being fruitful in every good work, and increasing in the knowledge of God" (Col. 1:10); "Wherefore leaving the word of the beginning of Christ, let us go on to more perfect things" (Heb. 6:1).

From these diverse passages St. Thomas draws out this opinion, which he expounds in his *Commentary on the Epistle to the Hebrews*, chap. 6, 2: "With regard to progress to perfection, a man ought to always strive to pass over to the perfect state." And to himself he makes an objection, namely: Perfection consists in the counsels, for it is said: "If thou wilt be perfect, go sell all things, etc." (Matt. 19:21), but not all men are obliged to the counsels. Therefore, as St. Paul says, "Let us go on to more perfect things."

St. Thomas replies (*ibid.*): "Perfection is twofold: one namely *exterior*, which consists in exterior acts (or commanded acts) which are signs of the interior acts, such as virginity and voluntary poverty. And to this perfection not all are held. The other is *interior*, which consists in the love of God and neighbor, according to that in I Col. 3:14: 'have charity which is the bond of perfection,' and to the perfection of this kind (that is, to the perfection of charity) not all are held, but *all are held to tend towards it*, because *if someone does not wish to love God more, he would not do what charity demands*." Whence St. Thomas here cites the saying of St. Bernard: "On God's road, not to go forward is to go back." — Likewise on Matt. 19:12: "He that can take, let him take it," St. Thomas says: "He who does not always will to be better, would not be able to will without contempt."

2. The aforesaid proposition *can be proved theologically* in two ways: a) from the precept of charity, and b) from the state of charity in the wayfarer.

a) **From the precept of charity:** (cf. II-II, q. 184, a. 3, argument "on the contrary," and read the corpus of the article at "Now the love of God...".) — From the fact that the first precept is without measure, "Thou shalt love the Lord thy God with thy whole heart, and with thy whole soul, and with thy whole mind": it follows that the perfection of charity is commanded as an end. From this is deduced, says St. Thomas, that "all, both religious and seculars, are bound, in a certain measure, to do whatever good they can, for it is said to all without exception: 'Whatever thy hand is able to do, do it earnestly' (Eccles. 9:10). Yet there is a way of fulfilling this precept, so as to avoid sin, namely, if one does what one can as required by the conditions of one's state in life: provided there be no contempt of doing better things, which contempt sets the mind against spiritual progress" (II-II, q. 186, a.2, ad 2).

The whole article 3 of q. 184, II-II, ought to be read with great attention and it virtually contains whatever we will say hereafter.

b) **It is proved from the state of charity in the wayfarer:** For the charity of the wayfarer of itself tends to the charity of the heavenly fatherland; just as grace is the seed of glory. St. Thomas says: "Charity when it will have been strengthened is perfected" (II-II, q. 24, a. 9). This supernatural life of charity is at first in the state of infancy, afterwards of adolescence, and finally of manhood. This tendency in itself relates to the nature of a road, otherwise the road would no longer be a road to a destination, but would be the destination itself. And he says upon Matthew's Gospel 7:13: "Broad is the way that leadeth to destruction and narrow is the way that leads to life"; now to walk spiritually is to advance (St. Thomas upon Eph. 4, lect. 6). — Again, in the Gospel, charity is compared to a seed or a grain of mustard seed, which ought to grow, or to the talents. And in this last parable it is said (Matt. 25:25): the Lord says of that man who had received one talent and had hidden it in the earth: "Take ye away therefore the talent from him, and give it him that hath ten talents. For to everyone that hath shall be given, and he shall abound: but from him that hath not, that also which he seemeth to have shall be taken away": from the one not bearing fruit he will take that which he has.

This is valid in different ways for beginners, for proficients, and also for the perfect, concerning whom St. Thomas says: "The more a thing approaches its end the more it ought to increase" (to the Hebrews, chap. 10, lect. 2).

Objection: Someone could object: This deduction is not valid, for St. Thomas himself says: "One does not transgress the precept, if one does not attain to the intermediate degrees of perfection, provided one attain to the lowest" (II-II, q. 184, a. 3 ad 2). Therefore not all Christians are held to tend to a greater charity than they have.

An answer is made to this from the consideration itself of the precepts (Barthier, *op. cit.*, 1, 317).

Firstly, the perfection of charity does indeed fall under the precept of charity, not as the matter, but as an end to be attained; otherwise that precept would have a measure, and that which would be more than this would remain only of counsel, which is against the precept's rule as is shown in q. 184, a. 3. Therefore all are obliged by the precept of charity not so as to be attained immediately, but as an end to which everyone according to his own condition ought to tend.

Secondly, to nowise dispose oneself to the advancement of charity would be to cease from every act of charity, which would be contrary to the precept; for all Christians are obliged to flee from sin, every sin either venial or mortal, but this cannot be accomplished without meritorious actions, by which the soul is disposed to advance, or rather grow, in charity. At least on the Lord's Day all Christians must hear Mass and perform acts of religion and charity towards God.

Thirdly, the precept of charity is the end of the other precepts which pertain to the means; but every Christian must fulfill these secondary precepts on account of the end of charity itself, and this cannot be accomplished without merit and by being disposed to advance. Therefore the precept of possessing at least the common charity involves the precept of tending to a greater charity.

Objection: But someone who produces only remiss acts of charity does not sin, on the contrary merits, and nevertheless according to St. Thomas does not advance.

Response: "Man advances in the way to God, not merely by actual increase of charity, but also by being disposed to that increase" (II-II, q. 24, a. 6, ad 3). So it happens by remiss acts, that they are meritorious, still inasmuch as they are remiss they are not sufficiently opposed to the inordinate passion, and under this aspect they dispose to sin, such that "not to advance is to go back"; to impede the growth of charity would be to sin against the precept of charity.

Third proposition: *Nevertheless no one is held to possess a charity which is uncommon or is proper to the perfect* (Cf. Barthier, 1, 279 ff.). For it suffices that a beginner tend to the charity of the proficients, and a proficient to the charity of the perfect, everyone according to his own condition; and in whatever spiritual age, there are many grades. Certainly it suffices for salvation that someone die in the state of grace, even in the lowest grade. — This is clearly said by St. Thomas in II-II, q. 184, a. 2, in which it is noted that the perfection which is necessary for salvation is that which excludes mortal sin. And in his Commentary on I Cor. chap. 3, lect. 2, St. Thomas says that "another perfection is of *supererogation*, when one adheres to God beyond the common state, which occurs by withdrawing the heart from temporal things," that is, by effectively observing the three counsels. The counsels do not oblige as do the precepts.

Fourth proposition: *Not all Christians are held to tend explicitly, that is by using the immediately proportionate means, to the perfection of charity.* Nor are all individually and immediately invited to this (cf. Barthier 1, 284; St. Thomas on the Epistle to the Hebrews chap. 6, lect. 1). But they ought to avoid all venial sins, grow in charity, and if they would do this they would be called not only remotely, but proximately to a high perfection, indeed they would be called efficaciously.

St. Thomas indeed teaches that the perfection of charity falls under the precept, but as an end to which one *should tend in some way*, namely, by growing in charity; it is not nevertheless necessary for each and every person to tend explicitly, namely, by using *the immediately proportionate means* to a high sanctity, which expresses a heroicity of the virtues, although we all ought, given the occasion, to undergo martyrdom rather than renounce the faith put in question (II-II, q. 184, a. 3).

Again, St. Thomas teaches that the gifts of the Holy Ghost are necessary for salvation, but he does not assert this with regard to the higher degrees of the gifts, nor with regard to the act of infused contemplation. All Christians ought to tend not to the effective practice of the three counsels, but *to the spirit of the counsels*, namely, *to the spirit of abnegation* (II-II, q. 68, a.2).

Whence the principle conclusion holds true: All Christians, everyone according to his own condition, is held to tend to a greater charity, always acting on account of the supernatural motive of charity, according to that saying: "All whatever you do in word or in work, do all in the name of the Lord Jesus Christ, giving thanks to God and the Father by him" (Col. 3:17).

Nevertheless, those sinning against the precepts do not commit a special sin against perfection, apart from other sins, because this obligation is general, and not special.

Whether every single Christian in particular is invited to keep certain counsels according to his own condition? — Yes, by all means: It is indeed very difficult to observe all the precepts if at least some counsels proportionate to each one's condition are not put into practice. These counsels lead one to avoid imperfections which immediately dispose to venial sins, and lead one to fulfill the good works appropriate for each person. And so some non-mandatory prayers are very useful, besides the hearing of Mass on the Lord's Day, which is of precept. Cf. Barthier 2, 219: "It is very rare for a Christian to be faithful to all the secondary precepts when he neglects the whole practice of the evangelical counsels."

Whether every single Christian in particular is invited to perform the general three counsels? — They are not. For not all are called to the religious life. But everyone ought to strive to have the spirit of the counsels, namely, the spirit of abnegation. For Christ says: "All men take not this word, but they to whom it is given. For there are eunuchs, who were born so from their mother's womb: and there are eunuchs, who have made themselves eunuchs for the kingdom of heaven. He that can take it, let him take it" (Matt. 19:12). About this passage, St. Thomas says (on Matthew): "That it is not expedient to marry is true for some men, but it is not true as regarding all, because not all have so much virtue that they may abstain; but to whom it is given, because to some it is given not from their own achievement, but by the gift of grace, according to that passage of Wisdom 8:21: 'I knew that I could not otherwise be continent, except God gave it.' For it is not of man to live beyond the flesh but of God" (cf. I-II, q. 108, a. 4, ad 1). It remains certain nevertheless, as St. Thomas says (*ibid.* on St. Matthew), that every man is held in his own condition "to (tend to) better things according to affection": (not according to act), "whence he who does not always want to be better, cannot want without contempt." (Cf. Rom. 6:3-13.)

Whence our principle conclusion remains certain: *All Christians are held to tend to a greater charity according to each one's condition.*

Corollaries:

1. In the way of God, not to advance is to go backwards, because there is a duty of advancement, just as for a child there is the natural law of growing, otherwise he becomes a deformed dwarf. Likewise, a chariot which remains too long in the stables is retarded.

2. The progress of charity ought to be accelerated: "The more a natural movement (e.g. of a falling rock) approaches the terminus, the more it increases. Now grace tends to follow the manner of nature, therefore the more they who are in the state of grace approach the end, the more they ought to grow in grace" (cf. St. Thomas on the Epistle to the Hebrews 10:25). (In another work, *The Love of God and the Cross of Jesus*, vol. 1, pp. 150-162, we have explained at length this corollary with its application to holy communion and to the progress of charity in the life of the Blessed Virgin Mary.)

3. If perfect charity is the end of the precept (or falls under the precept as its end), then ever more lofty actual graces are offered to us, proportionate to this end; because God does not command impossible things. Thus Christ said: "Be you perfect, as also your heavenly Father is perfect" (Matt. 5:48). Likewise, St. Paul said: "This is the will of God, your sanctification" (I Thess. 4:3); "He chose us in him before the foundation of the world, that we should be holy and unspotted in his sight in charity" (Eph. 1:4). — Whence we ought to hope for the attainment of this end, and not to say: humility prohibits one to tend to this height. Therefore perfect charity such as is found in the transforming union as the perfect preparation [disposition] for the beatific vision, is evidently the pinnacle of the normal progress of charity, or of baptismal grace.

We have shown sufficiently, therefore, that Christian perfection consists essentially in the precepts and that the perfection of charity falls under the supreme precept, not as its matter, or not as a thing to be immediately accomplished, but as an end to which all ought to tend, everyone according to his own condition; this man in the state of matrimony, another in the priestly life, or in the religious state (II-I, q. 183, 3).

Hence Christian perfection is only accidentally and instrumentally in the evangelical counsels properly so-called, as in the means for more easily and more quickly arriving at sanctity. But without the effective [actual] practice of the counsels someone in the state of matrimony is able to be a saint, as long as he has the spirit of the counsels nevertheless, and is prompt in observing them if they were necessary, e.g. for keeping absolute chastity after the death of his wife, or poverty in the case of ruin.

For the complete treatment of this teaching, one ought to note in comparing a counsel with a precept, that while a counsel is said to be "concerning a better good," this does not mean a good better than the work prescribed by the precept; for a lofty charity also falls under the precept as an end, and indeed martyrdom can be of precept, given the occasion; but "concerning the better good" wishes to say better than the opposed work freely chosen, namely:

—Poverty consecrated to God is better than the legitimate use of riches;

—Absolute chastity consecrated to God is better than the legitimate use of matrimony;

—Religious obedience is better than the legitimate use of our liberty.

This is confirmed from the division of the counsels given by St. Thomas in I-II, q. 108, a. 4.

Article 2.
Concerning the special obligation of tending to perfection for religious

State of the question: Here is treated of the *simple religious*, albeit he will have received no Order, such as the lay brothers and sisters or nuns. The question with regard to priests will be in article three. — It is also here treated concerning

perfection properly so-called, as is distinguished from the lowest
perfection which only excludes mortal sin, and from the middle
perfection which excludes fully deliberate mortal and venial sins
simultaneously, but not a remiss manner of acting. Whence here
is treated the higher perfection of the perfect which excludes
deliberate imperfections and a remiss manner of acting and
of receiving the sacraments and entails the observance of the
counsels and works of supererogation. — Finally it is treated
here *concerning the special obligation*, not only concerning the
general obligation. There is a notable difference between the
two, for, as we have said, there is already a general obligation
for all Christians of tending to a greater charity, and since this
obligation is general its violation is not a special sin distinct from
the sins arising from the violation of the precepts. Now however
it is asked whether there is a *special* obligation for the religious
of tending to perfection properly so-called, such that its violation
would be a special sin?

The general *answer* is: Religious are held by virtue of their
profession to tend to perfection properly so-called, through the
general means of the three counsels and the corresponding vows
of obedience, poverty, and chastity and through the particular
means of the rules of each Order or Institute.

To explain this doctrine, this special obligation will be studied
according to the four causes, namely: firstly, its foundation or
efficient cause; secondly, its nature or form; thirdly, its end;
fourthly, the matter about which it is concerned or the general
and particular means to the end; and fifthly its excellence shown
by its fruit.

* * *

Firstly, what is the foundation of this special obligation?
— It is the *religious profession*, by which the religious state is
constituted, which is the state of perfection: "Someone is said to be
in the *state* of perfection properly so-called, not from this, that he
has the act of perfect love, but through *binding himself perpetually*
with some solemnity *to those things which pertain to perfection.*

Moreover, it happens that some bind themselves to that which they do not keep, and some fulfill that to which they have not bound themselves... And so, nothing prevents some from being perfect who are not in the state of perfection (e.g. St. Benedict Joseph Labre), and some in the state of perfection without being perfect" (cf. II-II, q. 184, a.4).

Nevertheless the "state of perfection" is sometimes said not in a juridical and canonical way but in a spiritual way; in such a way St. John of the Cross many times speaks concerning the state of perfection as concerning a spiritual perfection.

St. Thomas speaks thus: "By inward spiritual growth a man reaches *the state of perfection in relation to the Divine judgment.* But as regards the distinctions of ecclesiastical states, a man does not reach the state of perfection except by growth in respect to external actions" (*ibid.* cited above, a.4 ad 1). Likewise: "There is required for the state of perfection a perpetual obligation to things pertaining to perfection, together with a certain solemnity. Now both these conditions are competent to religious and bishops. For religious bind themselves by vow to refrain from worldly affairs, which they might lawfully use, in order more freely to give themselves to God. In like manner, bishops bind themselves to things pertaining to perfection when they take up the pastoral duty, to which it belongs that a shepherd lay down his life for his sheep" (*ibid.* in art. 5).

And so religious are in the state of acquiring perfection, and bishops are juridically in the state of exercising perfection.

Simple vows suffice for constituting the state of perfection, according to the new law; Gregory XIII declared this.

But one must always recall *the supreme precept*, so that, as it is clear, religious life, which ought to aid perfect charity, or union with God and neighbor, is not diminished, but rather glorified, magnified, driven forward and vivified from on high. — Thus the religious life is directed by the great impulse of the three theological virtues and gifts, in fact not merely juridically but also spiritually. And it is evident that the three theological virtues (in which Christian life especially consists) are higher than the three religious virtues (in which religious life consists).

* * *

Secondly, what exactly is the nature or form of this obligation? — *It is a special obligation of tending to perfection*: "Men (religious) who enter the state of perfection do not profess to be perfect, but to tend to perfection. Whence the Apostle says: 'Not as though I had already attained, or were already perfect; but I follow after, if I may by any means apprehend...' (Phil. 3:2). Hence, a man who takes up the state of perfection is not guilty of lying or deceit through not being perfect, but through withdrawing his mind from the intention of reaching perfection" (cf. II-II, q. 184, a.5, ad 2). Likewise: "Hence it does not follow that whoever is in the state of perfection is already perfect, but that he tends to perfection" (q. 186, a. 1, ad 3). The same doctrine is likewise in article two; read attentively this second article: Whether every religious is bound to keep the three counsels? — He is indeed bound to keep the three evangelical counsels, but he is only bound to keep those exercises determined by his own rule. — If therefore a religious withdraws his mind from the intention of reaching perfection, he sins not only against the general obligation of all Christians to advance in charity, but also against the special obligation of the religious (cf. Passerini's Commentary, pg. 757, n.15). A religious nevertheless is not bound to actually reach perfection on the way, that is to say, before death.

First question: *Whether it would be a mortal sin for a religious to withdraw his mind from reaching perfection?* (Cf. II-II, q. 186, a.9.)

The answer is affirmative. Firstly, if a religious or even a simple Christian disdains the very tending to perfection; or secondly, if there is a transgression of the vows of profession in a grave matter, for this is precisely to withdraw the mind from the intention of reaching perfection. But a transgression of the exterior practices is not a mortal sin except either by reason of contempt of the rule, or by reason of the violation of a formal command whether given specially by the superior, or expressed in the rule. Reply to a first objection: Certain rules, such as the rule of the Order of Preachers, do not involve sin, either mortal or venial, but only to suffer the punishment affixed thereto. This is said per se, but *per accidens* it is frequently a sin of negligence, because if the rule is not kept this is due to an inordinate affection for some creature, just like the rich young man, who did not answer the Lord's calling since he was excessively attached to temporal things (cf. St. Thomas on Matthew, 19:21). Moreover, it is very rare that a religious would keep his own vows if in practice he neglects all the practices of his own Institute, just as a Christian very rarely keeps all the precepts if in practice he omits all the counsels (Barthier 1, 219).

Second question: *Whether the special obligation for a religious of tending to perfection is separate from his obligation of keeping the three vows, and whether this obliges gravely?*

Many theologians hold that this obligation is separate from the obligation of the vows, and it obliges gravely.

But the Thomistic and correct *opinion* seems to us to be that which is defended by the Salmanticenses, who cite Cajetan and many others as being in favor of it. The opinion is: *this obligation is grave, but it is not distinct from the obligation of keeping the vows.* Likewise, Passerini, p. 758, n. 14, and the Salmanticenses, *Moral Theology,* vol. 4, On the Religious State, p.4 ff., say:

1. "A religious is gravely bound to always tend to perfection, because it is the substantial and primary obligation of his own state, to which he has obliged himself by force of his profession." In what way is he obliged? "Such an obligation consists in a certain continual movement of tending to perfection, such that the religious never halts in this movement and progress, nor does he say, it is enough, but instead he always aspires to higher things, because in the way of God, not to advance is to go backwards.

"But this does not mean that a religious is held to tend to perfection by observing all the practices of counsel or of supererogation (cf. II-II, 186, 2), but by observing only those which are definitely prescribed to him by the rule he has professed. And hence follows: Firstly, that this obligation is not distinct from the obligation of keeping the vows and regular practices of the rule he has professed, but it is the same with it, or it is absorbed in it.

Whence there is not a doubled sin (cf. Cajetan on q. 186, a.9, and many others). From what has been said it follows: Secondly, that a religious cannot tend to perfection in a more perfect manner than by doing well those things which belong to his own state. And so they are more apt means of attaining to one's own end, and they lead to the height of perfection. Perfection is not, for example, to be found in extraordinary penances.

2. "When exactly does a religious sin mortally against this obligation of tending to perfection? — Firstly, from a transgression of the vows in a grave matter; secondly, when one disregards the counsels conducive to perfection out of formal contempt (q. 186, a. 2 and 9, ad 3); thirdly, when one transgresses the rule for the purpose of impeding perfection; fourthly, when one firmly makes up one's mind to nowise care about perfection, saying, "It is sufficient to remain in a lower state." Billuart holds the same opinion about one who would say, "It is sufficient to remain in the state of mediocrity in which I am"; fifthly, when one induces others by his bad example to lead a corrupt life, or to relax their following of the rule, which should be understood as pertaining to a grave matter.

* * *

Thirdly, what precisely is the goal of this special obligation? — This is explained by St. Thomas without any diminution, so that it can be seen that its fullness can only be found in intimate union with God in accordance with the virtues and gifts.

This is perfection itself, properly so-called, which consists in perfect union with God and neighbor, in accordance with imitation of Christ, namely, it is the perfect fulfillment of the first precept to which the evangelical counsels are subordinated.

St. Thomas explains this: "Religious bind themselves by vow to refrain from worldly affairs, which they might lawfully use, in order more freely to give themselves to God, wherein consists the perfection of the present life. Hence Dionysius says (*Eccl. Hier.* vi), speaking of religious: '*Some call them "therapeutas,"* i.e.

servants, *on account of their rendering pure service and homage to God; others call them "monachos,"*[1] *on account of the indivisible and single-minded life which by their being wrapped in,* i.e. contemplating, *indivisible things, unites them in a Godlike union and a perfection beloved of God"* (II-II, q. 184, a. 5).

Likewise, it is stated that perfection is essentially found in the precept of charity, to which the other precepts and counsels are subordinated (q. 184, a.3). "The religious state is like a holocaust whereby a man offers himself and his possessions wholly to God" (q. 186, a. 7).

A religious ought to attain to this perfection through imitation of Christ, as Christ is the way, the truth and the life: Christ as man was the most separated from the spirit of the world and the most united with God, having been consecrated to God in His whole human nature, in all His faculties and actions. Hence it is especially said of the religious: "For you are dead; and your life is hid with Christ in God" (Col. 3:3), and as St. Thomas explain in his Commentary on this epistle: "Do not savor those things which are of this world, because you are dead to the world; your life is hid with Christ, for Christ is hidden to us, because he is in the glory of God the Father, according to that which is said: 'O how great is the multitude of thy sweetness, O Lord, which thou hast hidden for them that fear thee...' (Ps. 30:20); 'To him that overcometh, I will give the hidden manna' (Apoc. 2:17)." —This life hidden in Christ is not perfectly found except in the mystical life.

And so every type of religious life, either active or contemplative, can of itself lead the fully faithful soul to intimate union with God, and to sanctity, such that this soul can immediately after death enter into heaven.

For in the active life, the genus of "religious life" is more excellent than its specific difference, which is to exterior works of mercy. For every type of religious life, either active or contemplative, tends of itself to the perfect fulfillment of the first precept (cf. II-II, q. 152, a. 4, where it is said, "Virginity is directed to the good of the soul in respect of the contemplative life") to which the counsels and rules are subordinated.

---

1 I. e. solitaries; whence the English word *monk*.

Hence in order that the goal of religious life be seen in a more concrete and complete way, it ought to be stated that Christ willed to restore in this life the triple harmony which was existing in the state of original justice as much as is possible, and which was restored in Himself and in the Blessed Virgin Mary.

For the state of original justice there was:

Firstly, **perfect harmony between God and the soul**, completely subordinated to Him by the three theological virtues, the corresponding gifts, and humble obedience.

Secondly, **perfect harmony between the soul and the body**, through perfect subordination of the passions to reason and the will, and subordination of the body to the soul, that is to say, through perfect chastity especially.

Thirdly, **perfect harmony between the whole man and exterior things**, which were created for the service of man. Thus was harmony descending from God to the lowest creature.

In place of this threefold harmony, after original sin, which destroyed the highest harmony and consequently the two others, came concupiscence of the eyes, concupiscence of the flesh, and the pride of life, namely, the immoderate desire for external things which are no longer a means of perfection but an obstacle, the immoderate desire for carnal pleasure, and the use of one's liberty without humble subjection to God.

Therefore to restore the original threefold harmony, Christ gives three counsels concerning the better good, namely, the counsel of abstaining in the use of licit things to more securely avoid excess and of using the world as though not using it. In other words, He gives the counsel of poverty, of relinquishing ownership or at least the use of external things, and of consecrating them to God. He gives the counsel of absolute chastity, of renouncing matrimony and of consecrating one's body and heart to God. He gives the counsel of obedience, of renouncing the use of one's own will and of consecrating it to God. These three virtues of poverty, chastity, and obedience are subordinated to the virtue of religion, from which the vows proceed. Thus the threefold harmony of the state of original justice is restored, in as much as this can be done:

triple Harmony of original justice	triple Concupiscence	three Vows: pertaining to licit abnegation
1. between God and the soul: perfect obedience 2. between the soul and the body: perfect chastity 3. between the whole man and external things which ought to serve him: perfect poverty	1. pride of life from which arises disobedience 2. concupiscence of the flesh, the desire for carnal pleasure 3. concupiscence of the eyes, the immoderate desire for external riches.	1. religious obedience consecrated to God 2. religious chastity 3. religious poverty

* * *

Fourthly, the matter about which this special obligation is concerned is treated. (This point is deduced from the goal.) Moreover, the triple separation and triple religious consecration is here treated. The matter about which this special obligation is concerned is: Firstly, *the evangelical counsels* of obedience, poverty, and chastity, as being the general, secure, and very useful means, although they are not necessary for arriving at perfect charity; and secondly, *the rules* of each Institute, as being the particular means accommodated to the particular purpose of each and every Order.

As far as the counsels are concerned, the three vows are essential to the religious state. These three counsels have been given by Christ the Lord: "If thou wilt be perfect, go sell what thou hast, and give to the poor and follow me" (Matt. 19:21); "There are eunuchs, who have made themselves eunuchs for the kingdom of heaven" (Matt. 19:12).

— The religious state is an exercise of tending to the perfection of charity, and so it requires two things, namely, separation and consecration: firstly, it requires that a man *separate himself* from those things that may hinder his affections from wholly tending to God (II-II, q. 186, a. 7) (negative aspect); secondly, it requires that "a man *wholly offer himself to God* as a perfect sacrifice or holocaust" (positive aspect).

— Now three things may hinder one's affections from wholly tending to God: attachment to external goods, or solicitude for them, which is removed by the vow of poverty; the concupiscence of sensible pleasures, and the control of wife and children which are removed by the vow of chastity; and the inordinateness of the human will, which is taken away by the vow of obedience.

—Likewise three things are suitably offered to God in order that a sacrifice may be perfect:

external goods which are offered through the vow of poverty;

the good of the body which is offered through the vow of chastity;

the good of one's own will which is offered through the vow of obedience.

— Therefore these three are essential to the religious state: both as being a state of separation from the world and as being a state of consecration to God (read article 7).

The three acts of the religious virtues are offered to God by the higher virtue of religion, to which a vow pertains and whose proper object is the worship of God; and so this life is a truly perfect sacrifice in imitation of Christ's life, and the religious who sins against the vows of religion commits sacrilege.

The virtue of religion, however, is commanded by charity, such that every religious act, whether it pertains to poverty, chastity or obedience, is by means of the virtue of religion ordered to the increase of charity and to its perfection.

See II-II, q. 88, a.6: where it is shown that it is more meritorious to do something in fulfillment of a vow, than without a vow: firstly, because in the former there is the merit of the higher virtue of religion; secondly, because thus a man offers to God not only an act but also the power, not only the fruit but also the tree; and thirdly, because by a vow the will is fixed on the good immovably, and so greater merit is obtained.

* * *

Fifthly, the excellence of the religious life is evident from its relation with the theological virtues by which we are united with God.

Poverty, which abandons all human helps, leads us to perfect *hope*, which is founded on the divine help, and so hope is a quasi-soul of holy poverty.

Chastity, which renounces sensible pleasures and conjugal love, leads us to perfect *love of God*, and so charity is a quasi-soul of *religious chastity.*

Obedience, which renounces one's own will and one's own judgment, leads us to the perfect life of *faith*, which in all things is directed by God Himself; and so faith is a quasi-soul of *religious obedience.* For the religious ought to obey his Superiors as to Christ the Lord, as to God speaking and revealing: just as Abraham, the father of the believers, obeyed God when he prepared himself for the immolation of his own son.

Such is the intimate relation between the three religious virtues and the three theological virtues as hope is the quasi-soul of holy poverty, faith is the quasi-soul of holy obedience; and charity is the quasi-soul of holy chastity.

This excellence of the religious life can be observed by opposition to the common state of the Christian life in three ways: firstly, in relation to God, Christ and the Church; secondly, in relation to the religious himself; and thirdly, in relation to one's neighbor.

Firstly, *in relation to God, the religious life is a state which gives more glory to God,* because one perpetually offers to God a perfect sacrifice or holocaust. The glory of God is the clear knowledge of God with praise; but God is more perfectly known and praised in the religious life, in which the words of the Lord's Prayer are fully verified: "hallowed be Thy name."

Secondly, *in relation to the religious himself, the religious life is more secure*, it frees more from sin, that is to say, from the concupiscence of the flesh, from the concupiscence of the eyes, and from the pride of life (Barthier 2, 202, 245). The vows indeed impose a new obligation, but they help more than they burden, just as wings for a bird (cf. II-II, q. 186, a. 10).

It is more *meritorious* because one who fulfills the counsels advances more in charity, which is the principle of merit.

It is a more *sanctifying* and *deifying* life, because it unites the soul more to God, and in all Orders and Institutes it can lead the faithful soul to more intimate union with God.

Thirdly, *in relation to one's neighbor, the religious life is more useful* than secular life on account of the *example*, on account of the *prayers and satisfactions*, for the religious ought to pray and satisfy for others, and on account of the various *works of mercy* both spiritual and corporal.

Article 3.

Whether clerics ought, by reason of their ordination and duty, to tend to perfection properly so-called, or in other words, concerning priestly perfection?

About this question, especially the following works are to be consulted:

In Sacred Scripture: The book of Leviticus chap. 11 and chap. 16; and among the Epistles of St. Paul, 2 Tim. 1:3-14, 2 Cor. 5:20, and to the Hebrews 7:26.

In the writings of the Fathers: St. John Chrysostom, *On the Priesthood*, especially book 6;

> St. Gregory the Great, *Pastoral Care*;
> Dionysius, *On the Ecclesiastical Hierarchy*, chap. 5, 2: PG 3, 507;
> St. Augustine, *On the Common Life of Clerics*, sermon 355: PL, 39;
> St. Peter Damian, *Opusc. 24, against the proprietary regular clerics; Opusculum 26, on the common life of canons*; Opusc. 28: PL, vol. 145, col. 511;
> St. Robert Bellarmine, *On Clerics*, chap. 27;

Thomassin, *The Old and New Discipline of the Church*, first part, book 3, chap. 2 ff. (Paris, 1725); vol. 1, pg. 1326.

In the writings of St. Thomas, especially II-II, q.184, a.8; and in the *Supplement on Holy Orders*, q. 31, 36, and 40.

The Council of Trent, sess. 22, chap. 1, O*n the Life of Clerics*.

The Roman Pontifical, the ordination of a priest.

Among the spiritual authors, *The Imitation of Christ*, book 4, chap. 5, "On the dignity of the Sacrament and Sacerdotal State";

— M. Olier, *Treatise on Holy Orders*; — *Life of St. Francis de Sales*, by the author Hamon, vol. 2, second part; — Cardinal Manning, *The Eternal Priesthood*; —Dom Gréa, *The Church*; —Cardinal Mercier, *The Interior Life, a Call to Priestly Souls*, (1918);

— Encyclical of Pius XI, *Ad catholoci sacerdotii fastigium*.

State of the question's difficulty: This state can be seen from a simple exposition of the diverse opinions opposed to each other. There are at least three diverse opinions, which at first glance seem to be completely opposed, yet they can indeed be reconciled, if I am not mistaken, in a higher synthesis according to the doctrine of St. Thomas, because they consider diverse aspects of the priestly life.

The first opinion is: A secular priest is not held to tend to perfection properly so-called, because he is not in the state of perfection, and in this he differs from a religious who has made his profession; nor is he in the state of exercising perfection, and in this he differs from a bishop.

So speak many secular priests, who view the priestly life more as canonists than as ascetics and mystics, and so they say, "We are not bound like the religious to evangelical perfection, nor to austerity, nor to the life of prayer, nor to similar higher things, since we are not religious." And thus sometimes excellent priests, hearing this theory which they suppose to be true, think that they are not able to arrive at perfection unless they were to leave their own ministry and enter the monastery. — So also many religious say: The secular priest is not properly bound to tend to perfection, because he is not in the state of perfection, nay it is very difficult for him to arrive at perfection if he does not enter into religion.[2] Then priests should abandon the people needing to be sanctified to find their own sanctification.

Second opinion: Every priest, even the one who is called "secular," is strictly bound to tend to perfection properly so-called by reason of his ordination and ministry in respect to the physical body and mystical body of Christ. Truly it would be very fitting that he be a religious, to make the three vows and to live in a community, just as the old canons regular, attached to a parish to exercise their own priesthood in a holy manner; for a priest ought not to be "secular." This expression is accepted by the Church, but it did not come from the Church, nor does it express the sacerdotal spirit.

And so according to Dom Gréa in his own treatise *The Church,* book 3, it is not fitting for a priest to be secular, but it is very fitting that he be a regular. Cardinal Mercier says something similar (*op. cit.*, pg. 155): "Secular priests, oh what an ugly word, secular priests." Nevertheless it can be said: He may be called secular not by reason of his spirit, but by reason of the occupations which materially are in the world [*in saeculo*]. Cardinal Mercier (pg. 189) prefers to use instead of the expression "secular clergy," these expressions: "diocesan cleric" and "diocesan clergy."

Third opinion: The secular priest not only ought to tend to perfection, but by reason of his own ordination and ministry, ought to be at least by participation in the state of exercising perfection, which strictly belongs to a bishop. Not only so, he would not become more perfect if he would enter religion, because he is already more perfect by reason of his Order and ministry than a simple religious who has not been ordained. Nay, he already is a religious, not of St. Dominic or of St. Ignatius, but by his own ordination he belongs to the order of Christ. Hence in the writings of Dionysius it is read in *Eccl. Hier.*, chap. 6, "The monastic order

---

2 Cf. regarding this first opinion Cardinal Mercier (*op. cit.*, pg. 163): "The religious infatuated [or in love] with their order or congregation do not always have a just appreciation either of the other orders nor of the place occupied by the 'secular' clergy in the ecclesiastical hierarchy. A venerable priest told me: 'They have more compassion than esteem for us.'"

ought to follow the priestly Orders, and by imitating them to ascend to divine things": (text cited II-II, q. 184, a.8; cf. Cardinal Mercier, *The Interior Life, a Call to Priestly Souls*, pg. 192).

Moreover, some add, as St. Thomas notes: "It is more difficult to lead a good life in the office of a parish priest or archdeacon than in the religious state. Therefore parish priests and archdeacons have more perfect virtue than religious," and not only more than lay religious, but also than religious priests (II-II, q. 184, a. 8, sixth Obj.).

St Thomas replies by distinguishing: "The difficulty that arises from the arduousness of the deed adds (of itself) to the perfection of the virtue (and it is greater in the religious life); but the difficulty that results from outward obstacles, does not add of itself to the perfection, but sometimes lessens the perfection, — for instance, when a man does not love virtue so much as to wish to avoid the obstacles to virtue; and sometimes it is a sign of perfect virtue, — for instance, when a man forsakes not virtue because of unavoidable impediments."

* * *

Solution: These three opinions consider the various aspects of priestly life. If we would wish, however, to consider these diverse aspects while at the same time following the doctrine of St. Thomas, it ought to be stated:

Firstly, *the "secular" or diocesan priest is not in the state of perfection simply* (neither of acquiring nor of exercising perfection) and he would have new merit if he would become a religious, on account of the vows of poverty and obedience (II-II, q. 184, a. 6).

Secondly, *he nevertheless ought to tend to perfection properly so-called, by reason of his ordination and ministry, for which a greater interior sanctity is required than the religious state would require* (cf. q. 184, a. 8).

Our first proposition harmonizes with the first opinion which views the priestly life from the exterior, just as a secular priest canonically is not simply in the state of perfection.

Our second proposition harmonizes under various aspects with the second and third opinions and it contains what is true in them.

According to this view, to be explained forthwith, there is a "special obligation" for the secular priest of tending to perfection properly so-called, which excludes, as far as human frailty permits, not only mortal but even deliberate venial sins and deliberate imperfections. This obligation in this view is not distinguished from the obligation of fulfilling as he ought, that is to say, worthily and holily, the various duties of the priestly life: the celebration of Mass, the recitation of the Office, the hearing of confessions, and generally the sanctification of souls. This special obligation is contracted in the reception of the minor and major Orders, and by force of the supreme precept these duties ought to be always better fulfilled.

The two parts of this thesis will now be proved.

First part: *The secular priest is not simply in the state of perfection.*

The "state of perfection," as St. Thomas shows, is not a merely an invisible state, just like the state of grace, but "a man reaches the state of perfection... by growth in respect to external actions" (q. 184, a. 4 ad 1). And it ought to be distinguished from the state of the perfect, which can be merely interior, just like the state of grace (as notes Cardinal Mercier, Pg. 165). From this St. Thomas deduces: "There is required for the state of perfection a perpetual obligation to things pertaining to perfection, together with a certain solemnity. Now both conditions pertain to religious and bishops. For religious bind themselves by vow to refrain from worldly affairs, which they might lawfully use, in order more freely to give themselves to God, wherein consists the perfection of the present life... In like manner bishops bind themselves to things pertaining to perfection when they take up the pastoral office, to which it belongs that a shepherd 'lay down his life for his sheep,' according to Jn. 10:15" (q. 184, a. 5). St. Thomas shows according to Dionysius that "bishops are in a position of perfecters, whereas religious are in the position of being perfected; the former of which pertains to action, and the latter to passion. Whence, it is evident that the state of perfection is more excellent in bishops than in religious" (a. 7). Hence theologians commonly distinguish the state of acquiring perfection, which corresponds to religious, and the state of acquired perfection, to be exercised and also to be communicated, which corresponds to bishops.

But, as St. Thomas demonstrates (q. 184, a. 6), secular priests (such as parish priests and archdeacons) are not simply in the state of perfection:

a) They are not simply in the state of acquiring perfection because, as the Holy Doctor says: "By receiving a certain Order a man receives the power of exercising certain sacred acts, but he is not bound on this account to things pertaining to perfection, except insofar as in the Western Church the receiving of a sacred Order (subdeaconate) includes the taking of a vow of continence, which is one of the things pertaining to perfection (as we shall state further on in q. 186, a. 4). Therefore it is clear, that from the fact that a man receives a sacred Order a man is not placed simply in the state of perfection, although inward perfection is required in order that one exercise such acts worthily."

But it can be said with Cardinal Vivès, *Ascetical Theology* (pg. 60 and 74), that on account of the vow of chastity a secular priest of the Western Church is *relatively* in the state of perfection; Suarez says: he is "inceptively in the state of perfection" (*On the Virtue and State of Religion*, book 1, chap. 17, n. 4). Likewise they are debarred from secular business.

b) Is he simply in the state of acquiring perfection? St. Thomas replies: "In like manner, neither are they placed in the state of perfection on the part of the cure which they (parish priest and archdeacons) take upon themselves. For they are not bound by this very fact under the obligation of a perpetual vow to retain the cure of souls; but they can surrender it, — either by entering religion, even without their bishop's permission (cf. Decret. 19, q. 2, can. Duae sunt),[3] — or again an archdeacon may, with his bishop's permission, resign his archdeaconry or parish, and accept a simple prebend without cure, which would be nowise lawful, if he were in the state of perfection...

---

3 Unless he be necessary for the diocese, cf. Code of Canon Law 512, 2.

"On the other hand, bishops, since they are in the state of perfection, cannot abandon the episcopal cure, save by the authority of the Sovereign Pontiff, to whom alone it belongs also to dispense from perpetual vows, and this for certain causes. Wherefore it is manifest that not all prelates are in the state of perfection, but only bishops" (ibid, a. 6).

Accordingly, a secular priest would have more merit if he were to become a religious, namely, the special merit proceeding from the vows of poverty and obedience. Wherefore St. Thomas demonstrates that a religious priest having the cure of souls is equal to the secular parish priest by reason of the Order and ministry or cure of souls, and is superior by reason of his state on account of "the goodness of the (perpetual) religious state," in which the religious binds his whole life to the pursuit of perfection. "Wherefore," he says, "the comparison of the religious state with the office of a parish priest is like the comparison of a holocaust with a sacrifice, which is less than a holocaust" (q. 184, a. 8).

"This comparison, however," says the holy Doctor, "must be considered as regarding the genus of the deed; for as regards the charity of the doer it happens sometimes that a deed which is of less account in its genus is of greater merit if it be done out of greater charity." So some secular priest, such as the Curé d'Ars, can be much more perfect than many religious and bishops.

"On the other hand," adds St. Thomas, "if we consider the difficulty of leading a good life in religion, and in the office of one having the cure of souls, in this way it is more difficult to lead a good life together with the cure of souls, on account of the outward dangers: although the religious life is more difficult as regards the genus of the deed, by reason of the strictness of religious observance" (ibid.). "The difficulty that arises from outward obstacles does not in itself add to the perfection of virtue, but sometimes lessens the perfection, — for instance, when a man loves not virtue so much as to wish to avoid the obstacles to virtue: sometimes it is a sign of perfect virtue, — for instance, when a man overcomes obstacles occurring unexpectedly or necessarily" (Cf. ibid. ad 6).

Hence the secular priest, but canonically speaking, *is not in the state of either acquiring or exercising perfection.*

* * *

Second part: *A secular priest ought to tend to perfection properly so-called, by reason of his ordination and ministry,* nay a *greater* interior *sanctity* is required for the celebration of Mass and for the sanctification of souls, than the religious state requires in a lay religious or in a monk. "You are the salt of the earth. But if the salt lose its savour, wherewith shall it be salted? It is good for nothing any more but to be cast out, and to be trodden on by men. You are the light of the world" (Matt. 5:13).

This proposition is proved in three ways: *a*) by reason of his ordination, *b*) by reason of his ministry pertaining to Christ's sacramental body, and *c*) by reason of his ministry to Christ's mystical body. (Cf. Passerini, *op. cit.*, pg. 104, n. 26 and 28, pg. 106, n. 33.)

a) **By reason of his ordination:** This is contained in the Roman Pontifical, in the ordination of a priest: "The Lord chose the seventy-two, thus teaching, both by word and by deed, that the ministers of His Church should be both perfect in faith and action; that is, well grounded in the virtue of the twofold love of God and neighbor," and in like manner writes St. Thomas in IV Sent. dist. 24, q. 2 (cf. Cardinal Mercier, *op. cit.*, pp. 200, 140, and 167). — This is clear firstly, from the prerequisites for ordination, secondly, from its effects, and thirdly, from its consequences.

Firstly, the state of grace, capability, and a goodness of life superior than is required for entering religion *are required for ordination:* "Holy Orders prerequire holiness, whereas the religious state is a school for the attainment of holiness. Hence the burden of Orders should be laid on the walls when these are already seasoned with holiness, whereas the burden of religion seasons the walls, i.e. men, by drawing out the damp of vice" (cf. St. Thomas in Suppl., q. 189, a.1 ad 3). This teaching is found in St. Gregory and in Dionysius (*Eccl. Hier.*, in the middle of chap. 5), having been cited by St. Thomas. In accordance with which, Fr.

Barthier says (2, 209), it seems that the level of charity appropriate
for receiving the priesthood is the level of the illuminative life,
so that in fact the priest having already been purified from sin
may be able to illumine others, while the level of the purgative
life suffices for entering religion; the level of the unitive life is
suitable for a bishop, because he ought to already be perfect and
perfecting. (Cf. also II-II, q. 184, a. 7 and 8, and Suppl., q. 40, a. 4
"*sed contra.*") Dionysius says, "The priestly power extends only to
cleansing and enlightening, but the episcopal power extends both
to this and to perfecting (cf. Passerini, pg. 82; summary, n. 2).

Secondly, *the effects of ordination* are *the character* and
sacramental grace. And the priestly character is a certain
participation in Christ's own priesthood, and since it is indelible,
it makes one a priest for eternity (cf. Suppl., q. 35, a. 2 and III, q.
63, a. 3). Whence, the priest ought to live as a worthy minister of
Christ. To this end sacramental grace is bestowed upon him by his
ordination: "The works of God are perfect. Consequently whoever
receives power from above receives also those things that render
him competent to exercise that power... (Hence) just as sanctifying
grace is necessary that a man receive the sacraments worthily; so
is it that he may dispense them worthily..." (*Summa* Suppl., q.
35, a. 1). And it is said: "The worthy exercise of Orders requires
not any kind of goodness but excellent goodness, in order that as
they who receive Orders are set above the people in the degree of
Order, so may they be above them by the merit of holiness. Hence
they are required (for ordination) to have the grace that suffices
to make them worthy members of Christ's people, but when they
receive Orders they are given a yet greater gift of grace, whereby
they are rendered apt for greater things" (*ibid.,* ad 3). These words
of the Supplement are not expressly from the hand of St. Thomas,
but something equivalent is read in IV Sent. dist. 24, q. 2: "Those
who are devoted to the divine ministry gain a royal dignity and
ought to be perfect in virtue," and this is also contained in the
Pontifical.

For when God calls a man to a higher end, He gives the
proportionate means to this end, and so the priest by virtue of
his ordination, if he does not demerit, has the right to new actual

graces so that he may holily exercise the offices of his priesthood. "Sacramental grace does confer, over and above sanctifying grace commonly so-called, and in addition to the virtues and the gifts, a certain divine assistance in obtaining the end of the sacrament" (cf. III, q. 62, a. 2). Sacramental grace is a new intrinsic mode, a special strength of sanctifying grace, with a right to the help to be bestowed in due time. Thus teach John of St. Thomas, Contenson, and Billuart on III, q. 62, a. 2.

Thus priestly ordination is a thing of greater dignity than the religious profession, as it confers a certain participation in Christ's priesthood, which is not found in a simple religious, e.g. a lay brother or in a monk. And so a cleric, receiving ordination, says in a manner of a promise: "The Lord is the portion of my inheritance and of my cup: it is thou that wilt restore my inheritance to me."

Thirdly, *a consequence of this ordination* is the special obligation of tending to a higher perfection as stated in the Pontifical. The bishop says at the end: "Dearly beloved sons, consider attentively the Order you have taken, and the burden laid on your shoulders. Endeavor to lead a holy and godly life, and to please almighty God, that you may obtain His grace, which may He of His mercy be pleased to grant you." It behooves the priest to sanctify himself, so that the sacramental grace of the Order may always bear more fruit.

Now every Christian is already, as was said above, held to tend to a greater charity while he is in the way, therefore all the more the priest, so that he may more perfectly fulfill the precept: "Be you therefore perfect" and "For he that hath, to him shall be given, and he shall abound" (Matt. 13:12); and "You are the light of the world and the salt of the earth."

Hence in the *Imitation of Christ*, on the priestly state it is read: "Behold, thou art made a priest, and art consecrated to celebrate; see now that faithfully and devoutly, in due time, thou offer up sacrifice to God and that thou show thyself blameless. Thou hast not lightened thy burden, but art now bound by a stricter bond of discipline, and art obliged to greater perfection of sanctity. A priest ought to be adorned with all virtues and set the example of a good life to others" (book 4, chap. 5). — Thus the responsibility of the priest is great, such that many saints feared to receive priestly ordination.

* * *

b) **By reason of the ministry pertaining to Christ's sacramental body** this obligation of tending to perfection is more evident:

Firstly, *the celebrating priest* indeed bears the figure of Christ, he is an *"alter Christus."* Now Christ offered Himself as a victim for us. Thus in order that he be a minister conscious of his own ministry, and in order that he celebrate worthily and holily, the priest ought to be personally united in mind and heart to the High Priest and Victim. It would be hypocrisy, willed at least indirectly out of negligence, if he were to approach the altar without the firm will of advancing in charity (Cardinal Mercier, 165); therefore he ought to say more holily each day in Christ's name: "For this is my body — This is the chalice of my blood." And in each Mass, the priest ought to receive devoutly *Eucharistic communion,* so that his charity may grow more and more. Therefore, normally each communion of his ought to be substantially more fervent and more fruitful, because each communion not only ought to preserve charity, but also to augment it, and thus dispose us to receive Christ's body better on the following day. This is already true for the simple faithful, all the more is it true for the priest (cf. St. Thomas on Epist. to Hebr. 10:25).

Hence it is not surprising that St. Thomas says: "Inward perfection is required in order that one exercise such acts (of Holy Orders) worthily" (q. 184, a. 6); and: "For the most august ministry of serving Christ Himself in the sacrament of the altar, a greater inward holiness is required than that which is requisite for the religious state, since as Dionysius says (*Eccl. Hier.*, chap. 6) 'the monastic order must follow the priestly order, and ascend to divine things in imitation of them.' Hence, other things being equal, a cleric who is in Holy Orders sins more grievously if he do something contrary to holiness than a religious who is not in Holy Orders: although a religious who is not in Orders is bound to regular observance to which persons in Holy Orders are not bound" (q. 184, a. 8).

Secondly, a simple priest is not inferior to a bishop as to the Eucharistic consecration (cf. Suppl., q. 40, a. 4 and 5). The episcopacy is not, according to St. Thomas, a special sacrament, but an extension of the Order of priesthood. (Cf. below, pg. 21 ff.)

The sanctity required for the celebration of Mass, or that is at least very clearly suitable, is expressed in the *Imitation of Christ*: "A priest clad in his sacred vestments *is Christ's vicegerent*, to pray to God for himself, and for all the people, in a suppliant and humble manner. He has before him and behind him the sign of the cross of the Lord that he may always remember the Passion of Christ. *He bears the cross before him in his vestment* that he may diligently behold the footsteps of Christ, and fervently endeavor to follow them. *He is marked with the cross behind* that he may mildly suffer, for God's sake, whatsoever adversities shall befall him from others" (book 4, chap. 5, n. 3).

Thirdly, this is confirmed *from the official prayer of the Church* to which clerics are bound from the subdeaconate; this official prayer ought to be said worthily, attentively and devoutly, so that it illumines the intellect and inflames the affections. Thus the Divine Office accompanies the celebration of Mass, and is, as it were, the continuation of Christ's prayer, just as the sacrifice of the Mass is the continuation of the sacrifice of the Cross. It is the singing of Christ's spouse and the familiar communication with Christ. — According to the theologians the obligation of reciting each day the canonical hours is of ecclesiastical law. But already, by virtue and by reason of the ecclesiastical state, a cleric is bound to pray more often than a lay person, and so the daily recitation is something befitting to his own state. Hence this practice of praying according to a fixed ritual was in vigor in the Church from Apostolic times, and it is insinuated in the Epistle to the Ephesians 5:19: "Speaking to yourselves in psalms and hymns, and spiritual canticles, singing, and making melody in your hearts to God." This practice of daily reciting the canonical hours seems to have been of precept by the end of the fourth century. — The importance of this prayer is evident from the fact that all clerics in major Orders are bound to recite the canonical hours at least privately under pain of mortal sin. In order that one satisfy the precept of the hours, literal attention (to the meaning of the words) or spiritual attention (to God and to the thing petitioned) is excellent and it is fitting that all strive to have this. Nevertheless, the resolve being supposed, or the intention virtually remaining, of praying and worshipping God, a superficial internal attention as to the words suffices.

Hence, just as the just man lives by faith, so the priest ought to spiritually live *by the celebration of Mass* and *the recitation of the canonical hours*. The Mass ought to be the summit of the whole priestly life, from which flow rivers of living water (cf. Cardinal Bona, *On the Sacrifice of the Mass*, ascetical work).

* * *

c) **By reason of the priestly ministry regarding Christ's body** this obligation of tending to perfection is still more evident.

In the sanctification of souls, the secular priest shares in the cure of souls which firstly belongs to the bishop (q. 184, a. 6 ad 3). He ought to be the bishop's collaborator. And even though by this cure of souls the parish priest is not constituted in the state of perfection, nevertheless in order that he sanctify souls, he ought to have a certain perfection. This is declared by the Council of Trent: "There is nothing that more leads others to piety and to the service of God than the life and example of those who have dedicated themselves to the divine ministry... Others fix their eyes upon them as upon a mirror and derive from them what they are to imitate. Wherefore clerics, called to have the Lord for their portion, ought by all means so to regulate their life and their conduct that in dress, behavior, gait, speech, and all other things nothing may appear but what is dignified, moderated, and permeated with piety" (sess. 22, chap. 1). A priest is not obliged to poverty, but he ought to be without affection for earthly things, yea indeed giving freely the things which he has to the poor, obeying the bishop and being a servant of the faithful, notwithstanding the difficulties and sometimes calumnies.

The necessity of already having acquired this perfection is evident for preaching, for the direction of souls, and for hearing confessions.

For preaching God's word, so that the priest may in fact speak out of an abundance of divine love, nay rather, as Cardinal Mercier (pp. 196 and 217) observes, so that he may preach fruitfully, every priest ought to possess a certain contemplation of divine things, for, as says St. Thomas: "The active life in which a man, by preaching and teaching, delivers to others the fruits of contemplation... is built on an abundance of contemplation" (III, q. 40, a. 1, ad 2). In this the priest ought to truly be the light of the world and salt of the earth.

Likewise, for hearing confessions a certain perfection is already required, on account of the dangers of this ministry, and so that the confessor may prudently, wisely, and lovingly direct souls to a greater purity, faith, hope and charity. Moreover, souls can come to him who ask from him higher direction so that they may more faithfully follow the inspirations of the Holy Ghost.

Conclusion: For all these reasons, the secular or diocesan cleric *is held to a greater perfection than a simple religious*, e.g. than a lay brother or a monk (Cardinal Mercier, pg. 188). As St. Thomas has said: "A greater inward holiness is required for the priestly office" (q. 184, a. 8). For the simple religious is only held to tend to perfection, but every priest ought to already have a certain perfection. Every priest, in order that he be faithful to the grace of his ordination, ought to say with St. Paul: "I will spend all things and be spent myself for your souls" (2 Cor. 12:15).

In practice: Does it suffice in conscience for a priest to have a firm, efficacious intention concerning himself worthily fulfilling all the duties of the priestly life, even the most perfect and heroic ones, if the need arises, or is it further required to already possess in reality a certain personal perfection?

It is replied with Suarez and Cardinal Vivès: Although a certain personal perfection is most suitable and morally necessary for correctly and worthily exercising the function of sanctifying others, nonetheless it is not simply and by precept necessary that such perfection actually precede; but it is sufficient that this perfection be possessed in an efficacious intention of himself worthily fulfilling the offices of the priest.

In other words, this obligation of tending to perfection is not distinguished from the obligation of correctly fulfilling the priestly office, just as for a religious it does not differ from the obligation of keeping the vows. Thus the priest does not sin against this obligation of tending to perfection except by neglecting his own obligations regarding his own office.

The usual means to this priestly perfection are *meditation* and *mental prayer*, spiritual reading, the study of Sacred Scripture in relation to the spiritual life, visitation of the Most Blessed Sacrament, weekly confession, and spiritual exercises every year. All these things are necessary so that the priest may know not only the letter but the spirit of preaching the Gospel from the abundance of the heart (cf. the Encycl. of Pius XI *de Sacerdotio*). The custom of common life, priestly associations in view of perfection, and third orders are to be praised.

Regarding the ascetical life of the priest, cf. Cardinal Bona's wonderful ascetical tract *On the Sacrifice of the Mass* (Herder edition, pp. 28, 75, 179, 325, 326, and 402).

Ven. Fr. Chevrier, a priest of Lyons and friend of St. John Vianney, used to propose this table to his disciples:

The Priest Another Christ

"I have given you an example, that as I have done, so you do also."

Manger		Calvary		Tabernacle	
poverty		spirit of death and immolation		charity	
The priest ought to be:		The priest ought to be:		The priest ought to be:	
Poor	*Humble*	*To die*	*To be immolated through*	*To give*	*To give life to others through*
in house,	in spirit	to body,	silence,	body,	his faith,
in clothing,	in heart	to spirit,	prayer,	spirit,	his teaching,
in food,	*by respect*	to will,	labor,	time,	his words,
in ext. things,	to God	to reputation,	penance,	his goods,	his prayer,
in labor,	to men	to family	sorrow, death	health,	his example
in service	to himself	and to world		life	
The more someone is poor and humble the more he glorifies God and is useful to his neighbor.		The more the priest is dead to himself, the more he lives and gives life to others.		The priest ought to become like good bread.	
The priest is a despoiled man.		*The priest is a crucified man.*		*The priest is a consumed man.*	

Fr. Chevrier taught catechism for abandoned children, and in order that one be admitted to this catechism only three conditions were required: to possess nothing, to know nothing, and to be able to do nothing.

Spiritual conclusion: For the priest, the sacrifice of his life can be made in this way in the celebration of the Mass, according to a certain formula of Pius X; and a counterpart relative to the four ends of the sacrifice, according to St. Peter Julian Eymard:

"Whatever is the kind of death reserved for me by Thy Providence, O Lord, I accept that with my whole heart from Thy hands, with all its sufferings, pains and distresses, as the way of arriving to Thee. And by the acceptation, together with the unbloody sacrifice of Thy Son, I offer to Thee in anticipation the personal sacrifice of my life in compliance with the four ends of the sacrifice.

"In the spirit of *adoration* of thy Majesty, O Lord of life and death, who bringeth to the extremity of death and leadeth back to eternal life.

In the spirit of *reparation,* for all my sins, known and hidden, and for the punishment due for them.

"In the spirit of *supplication* to obtain all the graces useful to me for salvation, and for the apostolate, and especially the grace of graces of final perseverance.

"In the spirit of *thanksgiving* for all benefits received, for the gift of the Incarnation, Redemption, Eucharist, my Christian and priestly vocation; and that my death be the beginning of an eternal action of thanksgiving."

In order that this sacrifice be made more perfectly, as a preparation for the final sacrifice at the moment of death, the priest suitably prays for the following graces:

"O Lord, grant that I may see whatever my Christian and priestly vocation demands, in some way as I will see that immediately after my death, in the particular judgment. In Thy mercy, grant me the grace *that I may fulfill* with love whatever Thou dost expect of me for the salvation of souls, whom I ought to assist, and *that I may suffer* with generosity, whatever painful thing Thou hast permitted from eternity for my sanctification before I at last come to Thee.

"I especially beseech that I may labor with zeal for the salvation of all the souls, whom, according to Thy will, I ought to assist. To this end I unite the personal sacrifice of my life with the unbloody sacrifice of Thy Son, of infinite and superabundant value, and with the immense merits of the Blessed Virgin Mary."

Article 4.

How the episcopal state is a state of perfection.

This question is of some importance not only in itself, but also relatively to other things. For many authors from the consideration of the episcopal perfection determine what ought to be the perfection of a priest and what is required for perfection in general. If in fact these authors do not have the correct notion of episcopal perfection, they do not correctly resolve the aforesaid questions.

See 2 Tim. 1:3-14; Council of Trent sess. 23, c. 4, 6, and 7; *Pontificale Romanum*: episcopal consecration; St. Thomas II-II, q. 184, a. 5 and also a. 4, 7, and 8; q. 185, a.8; q. 186, a. 3, ad 5; q. 188, a. 1, ad 3; Passerini, on II-II, q. 184, a. 5 and 7 (p. 73); and Suarez, *On the State of Perfection*, bk. 1, c. 15 and 16.

This question is not without relation to these other questions: Whether the episcopate is a *distinct Order* from the priesthood and a distinct sacrament, conferring a distinct character, and whether it is an *extension of the priesthood* and its perfect compliment? — Some men, such as St. Robert Bellarmine, St. Albert the Great, and Scotus, say: It is merely an extension and compliment of the priesthood (see St. Th., Suppl. q. 40, a. 5).

St. Thomas proves this opinion thus:

Firstly, the sacrament of Order is principally directed to the consecration of the Eucharist and to the sacrifice of the Mass (Suppl., q. 37, a. 2 and 4). But regarding the consecration of the Eucharist, a bishop does not have a greater power than a priest, not even the Sovereign Pontiff. Therefore... Nothing is higher among the sacraments and in the divine worship than the

Eucharistic consecration, for the Eucharist is the end of the other sacraments, insofar as it contains the Author of grace.

Secondly, the episcopate, however, adds to the simple priesthood the power of ordaining, of confirming, and of governing a diocese. Hence the episcopate, on account of that which it adds to the simple priesthood, is not a distinct Order from the priesthood, but is its extension and most perfect compliment. In this way, by divine institution a bishop surpasses simple priests, not only on account of jurisdiction, but on account of the power of Order insofar as one can ordain and confirm.

This is confirmed by the Council of Trent (Denz. 958), for in reviewing the Orders, it only enumerates seven, the episcopate having been omitted. And moreover, he who is not a priest cannot validly become a bishop; while on the contrary, he who has not validly received the deaconate, but only the subdeaconate, can validly become a priest.

It is indeed *objected*: The episcopal consecration confers a special character, because it gives a special spiritual power of ordaining and confirming.

It is *responded*: For this it suffices that the episcopate be the intrinsic completion of the sacrament of Order; thus a special character is not conferred through the episcopal consecration, but the priestly character is extended through a real and physical mode to further ministries, just as in the ordination of a priest the priestly character for consecrating is extended to absolving, when it is said: "Receive the Holy Ghost, whose sins you shall forgive... etc."

And it suffices that the episcopate be the intrinsic completion of the priesthood in order that it confer grace, just like sacramental satisfaction after absolution. Hence, more probably the episcopate is not an Order strictly so-called nor a sacrament distinct from the priesthood, but it is the fullness of the priesthood.

The episcopal consecration not only extends the priestly character to new functions of ordaining, of confirming, of consecrating churches and chalices, and of governing a diocese; but it gives also a notable increase of the sacramental Order's grace. This is necessary so that the bishop may fulfill his functions, not only validly, but holily and always more holily; this sacramental grace is a permanent modality of habitual grace, conferring the right to ever new and higher graces, so that the bishop may exercise his functions better and more fruitfully.

Hence he ought to live more and more from this sacramental grace, so that it may fructify in him; without this he cannot be perfect. Thus this grace is at the same time personal and social, just as the capital grace in Christ and just as charity perfects a person and his relations to his neighbor. A bishop receives at least five talents which ought to bear great fruit. Thus the episcopate is truly the fullness of the priesthood. And so the episcopal perfection cannot be obtained, except by aspiring to a greater union with Christ and with the whole Christian episcopate under the direction of the Sovereign Pontiff, in the mystical body of Christ. This unity of the episcopate is his strength.

The episcopate ought to expect all things from the sacramental grace, by cooperating with it. Thus it will become more and more conscious *of the sublimity of Christ's priesthood*. A bishop is simultaneously, as a successor of the Apostles, a teacher (thus he has authority to teach), a pastor of the flock (thus he has ministry towards the faithful and simple priests) and a leader governing a diocese or his own Church (thus he has authority to govern). Hence he possesses the three powers of teaching, sanctifying, and governing, and he ought in the event of persecution to give his life for the defense of his flock.

* * *

Regarding the state of perfection: let us see firstly in what the theologians agree, and secondly, what is disputed concerning the requisite perfection in a bishop.

Theologians commonly teach with St. Thomas that bishops are simply *in the state of perfection*, since for this state is required a perpetual obligation to those things which pertain to perfection together with some solemnity; but bishops oblige themselves to those things which are of perfection, assuming the pastoral office, to which it pertains that the pastor give his life for his sheep: a certain solemnity of consecration is also attached simultaneously with the aforesaid profession (q. 184, a. 5). Secondly, it is certain that the state of bishops is *more perfect than the state of the religious,* because as St. Thomas, following Dionysius, says, "In the genus of perfection, bishops are in a position of perfecters, whereas religious are in a position of being perfected; the former of which pertains to action, and the latter to passion" (*ibid.* a. 7). Whence, Passerini says (*op. cit.,* p. 72 n. 10), that according to St. Thomas, the bishop's state is *a state of the actively perfecting,* whereas the state of religious is *a state of the passively perfected.* For a bishop ordains priests and governs a flock. And, as says St. Thomas (q. 185, a. 4. ad 1), a bishop would "be going back" if he wished to pass to the religious state, while he was yet useful for his flock. — These two conclusions are commonly admitted.

But it is disputed concerning this: Whether the episcopal state not only is a state of those perfecting, but also ought to be called a state *of exercising perfection* in this sense, that it essentially presupposes *an already acquired perfection*, already possessed in reality? In other words: Whether a bishop is held to already be perfect, by a perfection not only broadly, but strictly so-called?

There are two opposite opinions:

The *first opinion is of Suarez* and of many others; it is *affirmative,* namely, a bishop is held to possessing and exercising perfection. Why? This is because the episcopal state is superior to the religious state, which is only a state of acquiring perfection. For a bishop not only ought to purify and illuminate others, but also to perfect them.

St. Thomas does not in a strict sense say that a bishop is in the state of an already acquired and exercising perfection, but he does say he is in a state of actively perfecting; that the episcopal state is a professorship of perfection (q. 185, a. 8); and, "The episcopal state is not directed to the attainment of perfection, by rather to the effect that, in virtue of the perfection which he already has, a man may govern others" (q. 186, a. 3 ad 5).

The *second opinion is of Passerini* (*op. cit.,* p. 70 and 73) and of many others, is *negative,* namely, by reason of the episcopal state there is not perfection strictly so-called, already possessed in reality, but only *possessed in intention.*

The reason is, otherwise either the elevation of the notion of perfection strictly so-called would be lessened, which truly excludes all deliberate venial sins and deliberate imperfections, or if the true and high notion of perfection strictly so-called be preserved, there would scarcely be found bishops being equal to their office (cf. Passerini, p, 73, n. 18).[4]

Nay, Passerini rejects the distinction of the state into the state of acquiring perfection and into the state of exercising perfection, at least in Suarez's sense.

Why? Because Passerini says, either it is proposed concerning common perfection and improperly so-called, which excludes mortal sins, and in this way every state is a state of exercising perfection; or it is proposed concerning perfection properly so-called, which excludes all deliberate venial sins, and a bishop is not held to already have it, and there will be few who have attained to it (ibid. pg. 72, n. 9).

Passerini adds: "A bishop who is not perfect, even who is bad, does not cease to be in the state of perfection," (ibid. pg. 72, n. 15) just as a bad religious does not cease to be in his state. And on the other hand, religious of apostolic life exercise or communicate perfection.

The importance of this question in ascetical theology. — This question thus posited is of some importance in ascetical and mystical theology for determining what is required for perfection properly so-called. Some, such as Suarez, do not seem to have a high notion of perfection properly so-called; for him it

---

4 St. Thomas, in Matt. 19:21 (ed. Marietti, p. 261, a): "The state of perfection is twofold: of prelates and of religious, but equivocally, because the state of religious is for acquiring perfection; whereas the state of prelature is not for acquiring perfection for oneself, but for communicating the perfection possessed" (read the entire text). A bishop is related to a religious as a teacher to a student. Cf. page 79 below.

It is said that some persons asked St. Thomas: Who is to be chosen as Master General: and that he responded: He who is more prudent ought to be chosen as Superior; he who is more learned ought to teach us; and he who is more holy ought to pray for us.

does not require a great charity. And among the many arguments for proving this thesis, they say: bishops are in the state of acquired and exercising perfection, and thus they fulfill their office. Passerini, on the contrary, seems to have a higher notion of perfection properly so-called.

What is to be responded? — The better solution is evident, if the question is proposed in this manner: Whether it would suffice that a bishop have a **firm, efficacious intention of himself fulfilling** all the duties of his office, even heroic if the need arises, **or is he further bound in conscience to already be properly perfect?**

Our **solution** is obtained from the distinction between a certain perfection **prerequired in conscience** for accepting the episcopacy, and the higher and **most fitting** perfection to which a bishop ought **to tend** (cf. St. Thomas, on Matthew, 19:21 (ed. Marietti, pg. 261, *a;* cf. the footnote above on page 78).

Hence our thesis is, and it agrees with Passerini: Firstly, one is not held to be already properly perfect for accepting the episcopacy; secondly, nevertheless a bishop, by reason of his office and state, is more obliged to tend to perfection than a religious, and through more holy means; and thirdly, moreover it is very fitting and interests him very much to already possess perfection properly so-called for worthily fulfilling all the duties of his pastoral office.

The first part of the thesis is: *One is not held to be already properly perfect for receiving the episcopacy.* For, it suffices that he have the efficacious intention of himself worthily fulfilling all the duties of the episcopal life, even the most perfect and heroic, if the need arises.

This opinion is contained in the in the writings of St. Thomas in which he replies to this objection: "There are many prelates (that is, bishops, as it clear from the context) and religious who have not the inward perfection of charity. Therefore, if all religious and prelates are in the state of perfection, it would follow that all of them that are not perfect are in mortal sin, as deceivers and liars." —St. Thomas replies both on behalf of bishops, and on behalf of religious: "Those who enter the state of perfection do not profess to be perfect, *but to tend to perfection*. Hence the Apostle says (Phil. 3): 'Not as though I had already attained, or were already perfect; but I follow after, if I may by any means apprehend': and afterwards he (St. Paul) adds, 'Let us therefore as many as are perfect, be thus minded.' Hence (says St. Thomas) a man who takes up the state of perfection is not guilty of lying or deceit through not being perfect, but through withdrawing his mind from the intention of reaching perfection" (q. 184, a. 5 ad 2um).

Hence a bishop is not bound in conscience to already be perfect, with a perfection properly so-called, which consists in so great a charity that a man would always adhere to God and would always deliberately act from charity, excluding deliberate venial sins and voluntary imperfections. For that reason it is said concerning a bishop: "Because he himself also is compassed with infirmity and therefore he ought, as for the people, so also for himself to offer" (Hebrews 5:2-3).

Therefore Passerini speaks correctly. — This first part of our thesis is confirmed from this that it is taught by St. Thomas: Whether he that is appointed to the episcopate ought to be better than others? St. Thomas replies with canon law: it suffices to choose a good man, nor is it necessary to choose a better man. And he explains, saying: "He who has to choose or appoint one for a bishop is not bound to take one who is best simply, i.e. according to charity, but one who is best for governing... On the part of the person appointed, it is not required that he esteem himself better than others, for this would be proud and presumptuous; but it suffices that he perceive nothing in himself which would make it unlawful for him to take up the office of prelate" (q. 185, a. 3).

In his reply to the third objection he writes: "Nothing hinders one from being more fitted for the office of governing, who does not excel in the grace of holiness." As it is said: "There are diversities of graces, and of ministries, and of operations" (1 Cor. 12).

The second part of the thesis: Nevertheless, a bishop by reason of his office and state is more obliged to tend to perfection properly so-called, than a religious, and by holier means (Passerini, p. 74; cf. St. Thomas, q. 185, a.3 ad 2: "A bishop ought to aim at showing himself to be more excellent than others in both knowledge and holiness"). A bishop, just as a religious, ought to aim at perfection without measure in respect to the end, for perfection consists in the perfect observance of the precept of charity, which precept is without measure. And in this respect, as Passerini rightly says (p. 71, n. 6), the state of perfection does not allow differentiation. But:

Firstly, *greater is the obligation* of tending to perfection for a bishop, than for a religious. Why? This is because a greater interior sanctity is required for the functions of the pastoral office, lest the bishop impede the bearing of fruit of souls and the salvation of his flock. This obligation is likewise weightier in a bishop than in a religious of apostolic life, both because the cure of the flock pertains to him more universally and more principally, so that he cannot withdraw from it, and because he is the highest and principle minister both of Orders and of doctrine, and thus the bishop is the pattern of the flock, according to 1 Pet. 5:3. Hence a bishop sins more gravely than a religious if he works contrary to perfection.

Secondly, the difference of states is derived *from the difference of means* which are taken up, in which a bishop excels. For among the works of counsel some are according to their genus *more perfect*, and of this kind are to have such and so great cure of the of the salvation of one's neighbors, that one would pour out his life to procure it. Now to this a bishop is obliged by reason of his state, and this means is *in itself* superior to the practice of obedience and religious poverty. For charity towards one's neighbor is the greatest sign of the growth of charity towards God. "Love one another, as I have loved you" (Jn. 13:34); fraternal charity is the thermometer of the interior life.

As Passerini says: "To have the cure of souls as a principle purpose in life and annexed to it the contempt of the bodily goods, of one's own reputation, and of one's life, is a state far surpassing all others in perfection, and for this reason a bishop is constituted in a state more perfect than of any religious" (*op. cit.*, p. 93; summary n. 6). "This is also the mind of St. Thomas, who thoroughly proves that the bishops' state surpasses in perfection the religious state, not because bishops are actually perfect, but because they are perfecters, because without a doubt the office of perfecting others is a work in itself, and from its nature, sublime and more elevated than poverty, chastity, and obedience, that is to say, in those things which are of counsel, and is a more useful means to obtain perfection. And in no other state are so many saints found, as the Martyrology bears witness" (*Ibid.*, p. 94, 8).

Objection: But religious seem to be more perfect, at least in respect to poverty and obedience.

Reply: Although a bishop is not held to this instrument of perfection which is poverty, nevertheless "bishops especially are bound to despise all things for the honor of God and the spiritual welfare of their flock, when it is necessary for them to do so, either by giving to the poor of their flock or by suffering with joy the being stripped of their own goods" (q. 184, a. 7, obj. 1) Perfection does not consist in voluntary poverty, but voluntary poverty conduces instrumentally to the perfection of life. Hence it does not follow that where there is greater poverty there is greater perfection; indeed the highest perfection is compatible with great wealth" (q. 185, a. 6, ad 1um). And if a bishop does not have the vow of obedience, he is bound to give an excellent example of obedience to the Sovereign Pontiff, and to be in a way *the servant of the servants of God* which is frequently more difficult and more arduous than religious obedience.

Query: Passerini (op. cit., p. 95) inquires: Whether the episcopal state is superior to the religious state of apostolic life (the Order of Preachers or the Society of Jesus, which have apostolic life, even with the danger of death in the missions) and whether a bishop is greater than the teachers in theology[5] who instruct many other priests, than perpetual regular Prelates, such as Abbots and [Superior] Generals, upon whom rests the

---

5 Regarding teachers in S. Theology, St. Thomas says in Quodl. I, a. 14, that beneath bishops "teachers of theology are like principal artificers who inquire and teach how others ought to procure the salvation of souls. Therefore, it is absolutely better to teach theology and more meritorious if it is done with good intention, than to devote particular care to the salvation of this one and that, whence the Apostle says: 'For Christ sent me not to baptize, but to preach the gospel' (1 Cor. 1:17)."

cure of some whole Order, and who besides the burden on the cure of souls have the burden of the vows and of regular observance.

General conclusion: It is answered with Passerini: The proximate end and object of the episcopal state far exceeds the end of the religious state, even to the extent that the latter may oblige himself to works of charity, and this [superiority is shown] in three ways:

Firstly, in the universality of actions: For only a bishop can confer all the sacraments; only he consecrates Churches and the matter of the sacraments of Baptism and Extreme Unction; only he has the right to vote in defining matters of faith; and he possesses [the privilege] by his office that he be called to a Council for deciding those things which refer to governing of the Church. But these things are not competent to religious;

Secondly, in the manner of acting: because religious in the cure of souls are affiliated to the bishop as helpers;

Thirdly, in the obligation: for religious do not have the same obligation of exposing one's life for the sake of the faithful's salvation, as the bishop has.

Third part of the thesis: It is very fitting and it greatly concerns a bishop that he already possess perfection properly so-called to worthily and holily fulfill all the duties of his pastoral office. (Cf. 2 Tim. 1:3-14.)

As a matter of fact, a bishop ought not only to purify and enlighten others but also to perfect, for he ought to ordain priests, and govern them, and be the father of the faithful of his diocese, be they of whatever state, having excluded the privilege of exemption. Moreover he ought to exercise very frequently the most noble acts of the virtues for the salvation of his flock, and to have the disposition of withstanding greater and more difficult things for his sheep. — For the worthy fulfilling of all these duties, it concerns him very much to give time to prayer, so that he may deeply live from the faith and from charity, and may be able to speak to his flock from an abundance of holy love (cf. the life of St. Charles Borromeo, of St. Francis of Assisi and of St. Alphonsus).

It is not required that a bishop surpass all men in everything, otherwise one could not become a bishop unless he were a virgin;

nevertheless it is suitable that he surpass in these things which pertain the office of feeding the flock. For which reason it is not fitting that one undertake the episcopacy unless one be perfect.

Thus understood, this thesis does not lessen the elevation of the notion of perfection properly so-called, and this seems to be the opinion of St. Thomas.

* * *

First query: *Whether it is lawful to desire the episcopacy?* (cf. II-II, q. 185, a. 1). It seems that it is lawful, for St. Paul says: "He that desires the office of a bishop, he desireth a good work" (1 Tim. 3:1); now it is lawful and praiseworthy to desire a good work. Yet Augustine says: the office of a bishop "is unbecomingly desired" (*De Civ. Dei*, bk. 19, chap. 19). Some assert an equality, regarding lawfulness, between this desire and the desire for contemplation or the mystical union.

Let us see what St. Thomas answers. He says: to desire the office of a bishop, on account of the precedence in dignity and honor, is unlawful; but to desire to do good to one's neighbors, is in itself praiseworthy and virtuous. Especially this was praiseworthy in the primitive Church, in the time of persecution, because bishops were frequently destined to undergo more severe punishments. — But if there is not an urgent reason for it, it would be presumptuous that anyone would desire the office of a bishop, because the episcopal act has the height of degree attached to it. Wherefore, some men make a vow of not accepting the office of a bishop unless by force of obedience or by the necessity of charity.

Nevertheless anyone may, without presumption, desire the office of a bishop "so that the object of his desire is the good work and not the precedence in dignity."

There is not an equality with the desire for the mystical union, because this union does not necessarily have an external height of degree attached to it, but very many painful purifications.

Second query: *Whether it is lawful for a man to refuse absolutely an appointment to the episcopate?* (q. 185, a. 2). — St. Thomas answers negatively: "Just as it is a mark of an inordinate will that a man of his own choice incline to be appointed to the government of others, so too it indicates an inordinate will if a man definitively refuse the aforesaid office of government in direct opposition to the appointment of his superior; because this is contrary to the love of our neighbor, for whose good a man should offer himself according as place and time demand. And secondly, this is contrary to humility, whereby a man submits to his superior's commands."

Third query: *Whether a bishop may lawfully forsake the episcopal cure, in order to enter religion?* He cannot do this unless with the permission of the Sovereign Pontiff and because he is hindered from procuring the spiritual welfare of his subjects, e. g. because he is old, or infirm, or on account of some scandal, or some defect in his subjects.

The reason is that "the perfection of the episcopal state consists in this: that for love of God a man binds himself to work for the salvation of his neighbor, wherefore he is bound to retain the pastoral cure so long as he is able to procure the spiritual welfare of the subjects entrusted to his care: a matter which he must not neglect, — neither for the sake of the quiet of contemplation, nor for the sake of avoiding any hardship or of acquiring any gain whatsoever" (q. 185, a. 4). "So long as a man can be useful to the salvation of his neighbor, a bishop would be going back, if he wished to pass to the religious state, to busy himself with his own salvation" (*ibid.* ad 1um).

Hence as St. Thomas says, "When the salvation of his subjects demands the personal presence of the pastor, the pastor should not withdraw his personal presence from his flock, neither for the sake of some temporal advantage, nor even on account of some impending danger to his person, since the good Shepherd is bound to lay down his life for his sheep" (q. 185, a. 6).

* * *

Confirmation of the necessity for the priest of tending to perfection:

Concerning the world in which the priest is obliged to exercise his ministry.

Christ said to the Apostles: "Behold I send you as sheep into the midst of wolves. Be ye therefore wise as serpents and simple as doves. But beware of men. For they will deliver you up in councils, and they will scourge you in their synagogues" (Matt. 10:16-17). — Likewise it is written: "Behold I send you as lambs among wolves" (Luke 10:3).

Likewise in I John it is said what is the spirit of the world insofar as it is opposed to the spirit of God: "The whole world is seated in wickedness" (5:19); "For all that is in the world, is the concupiscence of the flesh, and the concupiscence of the eyes, and the pride of life" (2:16).

St. Paul says: "Put you on the armour of God that you may be able to stand against the deceits of the devil. For our wrestling is not (only) against flesh and blood; but against principalities and powers, against the rulers of the world of this darkness, against the spirits of wickedness in the high places. Therefore, take unto you the armour of God, that you may be able to resist in the evil day and to stand in all things perfect" (Eph. 6:11-13).

The Commentary of St. Thomas on Matthew 10:16 says: "Why did the Lord so will to send (the Apostles) into dangers? This was for the manifestation of His power, because if he had sent some armed men, that might be attributed to His violence, and not to God's power; therefore He sent poor men. For it was a great thing that through poor men, both despised and unarmed, so many will have been converted to the Lord." St. Thomas, in his Commentary on Ephesians 6:12, observes that our principle weapons against the devil's wickedness are the three theological virtues: the shield of faith, hope of our final end, which is like a helmet of salvation, and the love of God and of souls, combined with humility and the spirit of adoration.

But I would like to speak in particular about the corruption of the world to be evangelized, not as it was in the beginning of the life of the Church, but as it is now after nearly twenty centuries of Christianity; for there is a notable difference between the two. Nowadays the large ideas of Christianity for many men have lost their loftiness, and so they have taken an absolutely different meaning. Thus many, such as Chesterton,[6] have rightfully spoken *about the large ideas having fallen down into insanity*; this began in particular with Jean Jacques Rousseau, whose teaching is rightly called *Corrupted Christianity*.[7] The corruption of the best men is the worst.

In classical antiquity there indeed already was great opposition between the spiritualism of Plato and Aristotle and the materialism of Epicurus. But the mind had not yet arrived at the loftiness of Christianity, and the higher philosophers were speaking only about wisdom and about some rational love of the Highest Good; and the Stoics were speaking about some universal fraternity of all men.

With Christianity the human mind was elevated to the supernatural life, according to a most certain faith in God, a most firm hope in Him, and a charity towards the heavenly Father and towards all His adoptive children. For three centuries martyrs died for the Christian faith, and the blood of the martyrs was the seed of Christians. The teaching of the Fathers was brought to its perfection by St. Augustine. Sacred theology attained to its peak in the thirteenth century.

Then there began the decline in the fourteenth century with Nominalism; in the fifteenth and sixteenth centuries with Protestantism, by the negation of the infallibility of the Church, of the sacrifice of the Mass, of the sacrament of Penance, and of the necessity of good works. The decline was still more powerful with the incredulous philosophers of the eighteenth century, Voltaire and Rousseau; with the French Revolution came the spirit of Naturalism after the mind of the Deists: 'If God exists He does not care about individuals but only about universal laws; henceforth sin is not an offense against God, but only an act against reason,

---

6　*Heretics.* Preface by H. Massis. "Les grandes idées devenues folles" (The great ideas have become follies).

7　Cf. J. Maritain: *The Three Reformers*, Rousseau: The corrupted Christianity.

which is always evolving; that which previously seemed to us to be theft, now is not theft; perhaps it is private property itself which is the theft,' as say the Socialists.

According to the spirit of Naturalism and Rationalism, all supernatural mysteries of the Most Holy Trinity, the Incarnation, the Redemption, the Eucharist, and the other sacraments are to be denied; the life of grace, the seed of glory, is to be denied; eternal life and the opposition between heaven and hell are to be denied.

In this decline at any one time Liberalism wishes to remain at a middle height between Catholicism and the worse errors. But Liberalism concludes nothing, and it neither affirms nor denies, but it fluctuates. Thus when a decision is to be made and when something is to be done, in the place of Liberalism comes Radicalism in its denial, then Socialism and finally Materialistic Communism, with its denial of property, family, country, and religion.

Some ideology remains which began with J. J. Rousseau, in which is found the corrupted Christianity after the mind of Naturalism, with the denial of all supernatural mysteries, and in the place of faith in God, of hope in God, and of charity towards God, is put faith in humanity, hope in humanity, and love of humanity (it is the phraseology of love, the art of making phrases about love). Humanity is put in the place of God and is deified. Consequently they always speak about the progress of humanity, as if there always was scientific, economic, moral and spiritual progress, as if humanity of itself, without higher help, could move itself to this progress.

Now we see with the present World War, and with the material progress of science and of the means of destruction, a terrible moral regression to barbarism, and at the same time an economic regression to misery.

Hence this new ideology, which is put in the place of Christian faith, contains large ideas fallen down into insanity. And the fall is so much more profound and rapid as it comes from a greater height, just as in the acceleration of a stone's fall.

Therefore the present state seems worse than it was before Christ. There is not the ignorance of a child, but the insanity of an old man, who had great culture. And thus it is not surprising that modern philosophers, who proceed according to the spirit of rationalism, are true intellectual monsters, such as Kant, Fichte, and Hegel. Spinoza had already begun denying God's liberty, creation, providence, God's justice and mercy, and all merit and demerit.

This is exactly the *foolishness* or *insanity* of which St. Paul spoke when he said: *"For the wisdom of this world is foolishness with God"* (1 Cor. 3:19). True wisdom judges both speculatively and experimentally about all things, even the lowest things, through the highest cause and ultimate end, while foolishness and insanity judges about all things, even about the highest things, through that which is the lowest, and in this way puts in the place of God the concupiscence of the flesh, the concupiscence of the eyes, and the pride of life. (Cf. St. Th. II-II, q. 46, on folly.)

CHAPTER II

ON THE LOFTINESS OF CHRISTIAN PERFECTION
to which especially priests ought to tend.

Not rarely, even in ascetical books, there is a discussion about Christian perfection in an exceedingly abstract way, by an enunciation of virtues which are required for it, insisting indeed on the perfection of charity. But in this way it is not shown concretely and vividly enough that in which this perfection of charity consists, and in which it differs from the charity of beginners and of proficients.

On the contrary, the great loftiness of Christian perfection appears in a very concrete and lifelike way, if we have before our eyes the beginning of the Lord's Sermon on the beatitudes, in the account of Matthew (5:2), and in the account of Luke (6:20).

Christ, at the beginning of His preaching, began to speak of beatitude, because all men naturally desire beatitude, but they often err by seeking this beatitude where it is not, namely, in sensible pleasure, in riches, in honors, in power, and in this way they are deceived by the concupiscence of the flesh, by the concupiscence of the eyes, and by the pride of life. Christ, on the contrary, shows exactly where is true beatitude, begun in this life and consummated after death.

Again St. Thomas begins his exposition of moral theology in I-II by the tract on the ultimate end and on beatitude, because the end is prior in intention, and last in execution (tract on the Last Things).

Hence, in like manner, spiritual theology ought to insist on the loftiness of Christian perfection, by showing it not only theoretically in the abstract, but in a concrete and lifelike way, following the Lord's words themselves. In this way it will be clear that the contemplation of the mysteries of the faith and the intimate union with God pertain to it; and the distinction between this Christian perfection and the charity of beginners and of proficients will be manifested.

This is especially necessary when there is discussion about the perfection to which priests ought to tend, as they are distinguished from the simple faithful.

Regarding this it ought to be observed with St. Augustine on the Lord's Sermon on the Mount, that in the account of Luke (6:20) there are four beatitudes, and in the account of Matthew (5:2) there are eight. In the account of Luke four are lacking, namely, blessed are the meek, the merciful, the clean of heart, and the peacemakers.

St. Augustine explains this, saying: "Jesus firstly ascended the mountain and made this sermon to the disciples, and afterwards descending He found the multitude gathered, to whom He preached the same things and recapitulated many things."

Hence it seems that this sermon was made in its fullness and loftiness for the Apostles themselves, and therefore that it especially is valid for priests.

Moreover, it ought to be observed that in each beatitude is found both a merit and a reward, begun at first in the present life and consummated after death. These merits, according to St. Augustine and St. Thomas, are acts of perfect virtues with the help of the gifts, e.g. of the virtue of fortitude with the help of the gift of fortitude, of the virtue of meekness with the help of the gift of piety, of prudence with the help of the gift of counsel, etc., and the reward having already begun shows the intimate union with God, which afterwards will be consummated in heaven. In this way nothing is more concrete for the describing of Christian perfection to which the priest especially ought to tend, so that he may direct the faithful to it.

St. Thomas, following St. Augustine, explains these beatitudes in his Commentary on Matthew, 5, and in I-II, q. 69.

The Beatitudes imply	an approach to the good	Bl. are they that suffer persecution,	all gifts and perfect virtues,
		Bl. are the peacemakers,	the gift of wisdom
		Bl. are the clean of heart,	the gift of understanding
		Bl. are the merciful,	the gift of counsel
		Bl. are they that hunger and thirst after justice	the gift of fortitude
	a withdrawal from evil	Bl. are they that mourn	the gift of knowledge
		Bl. are the meek	the gift of piety
		Bl. are the poor	the gift of fear

In the account of Matthew, just as in the account of Luke, the beatitudes are enumerated according to an ascending gradation, from the beatitude of poverty to the beatitude of those who suffer persecution, while on the contrary, in the passage of Isaias (11:2), the enumeration of the gifts descends from the highest gift of wisdom to the lowest, namely, of fear.

In like manner, in the Lord's Prayer the petitions are enumerated from the higher ones: "Hallowed be Thy name" to the lowest one "but deliver us from evil." This is pointed out by Augustine so that the correlation of the beatitudes might be better seen.

St. Thomas observes that by ascending in this way, *the three first* beatitudes involve a **withdrawal from evil**, blessed are the poor, the meek, and they that mourn; *the others* involve a **drawing near to the good and the best**.

Between them, are firstly enunciated *the beatitudes of the active life*, namely, "Blessed are they that hunger and thirst after justice" and "Blessed are the merciful."

Thereafter are expressed *the beatitudes of the contemplative life,* namely, "Blessed are the clean of heart" and "Blessed are the peacemakers," which are not in the account of Luke.

Finally there is the *summit*: namely, "Blessed are they that suffer persecution for justice' sake." It is the summit of Christian perfection, which especially appears in martyrdom.

The eight degrees of the ascent are excellently explained by St. Thomas in his Commentary on Matthew and in I-II, q. 69, a.3.

While the world says: happiness is in an abundance of exterior goods, in pleasure, and in honors; Jesus says: *Blessed are the poor in spirit, for theirs is the kingdom of heaven.* That is, in regard to riches and honors, blessed are those who use them moderately, or even despise them. This beatitude proceeds from humility and from the gift of fear in opposition to cupidity, envy and the spirit of pride. In this manner, all who aspire to perfection ought to tend to the spirit of evangelical poverty; even if they were to have riches, they ought to nourish in themselves the spirit of abnegation, especially priests. For the perfection of charity can be without the effective practice of the counsels, but not without their spirit.

Likewise, while the world says: blessed are those who have dominion over others; Jesus says: *Blessed are the meek, for they shall possess the land*; that is, blessed are those who do not get angry, who do not desire revenge in respect to their enemies, or dominion over them, but dominion over their irascible passions, so that the soul is rendered totally tranquil contrary to them. — This merit comes forth from kindness and from the gift of piety; because according to this gift we consider God as a father and men as brothers to be treated with kindness.

In like manner, while the world says: blessed are those who find consolation in pleasures and in vanities; Jesus says: *Blessed are they that mourn, for they shall be comforted*; that is, blessed are those who mourn over their own sins, and know that true evil is nothing other than mortal sin, which is the death of the soul; these find consolation infinitely superior to the delights of the world. These men use the concupiscible passions very moderately in the spirit of penance and according to the gift of knowledge, by which is known the vanity of earthly things and the gravity of sin (II-II, q. 9, a. 4). Knowledge is the cognition of things not through the supreme cause, but through the secondary defectible and deficient causes. A priest ought to be a penitent and ought to well receive penitents, and to move them to true and persevering penitence.

In this way these three previous beatitudes imply a withdrawal from evil (as in the purgative way). — The two following ones imply an approach to the good, and they pertain to the active life (they are exercised in the way of the proficients).

Pride says: blessed is he who lives and acts as he wishes, who is subject to no one, and who presides and has dominion; Jesus, on the contrary, says: *Blessed are they that hunger and thirst after justice, for they shall have their fill.* This beatitude, according to St. Augustine and St. Thomas, corresponds to the gift of fortitude by which difficulties are continually overcome and the ardor of the love of justice or perfection is preserved, even amidst adversities, unto old age. Then it is evident that the thirst and hunger for justice are not only an ardor of sensibility, or an inflaming of soul which quickly passes and is conquered.

But as love of justice ought to be united with the love of mercy, just as in God, accordingly it is immediately said: Blessed are the merciful, for they shall obtain mercy, namely, blessed are they who do not oppress their subjects, and who are good counselors for the benefit of the afflicted, to them God will show mercy. This beatitude, according to St. Augustine and St. Thomas, corresponds to the gift of counsel, because mercy inclines to bestowing good counsel to the afflicted, and because when the mind hesitates between the way of justice and the way of mercy, the Holy Ghost inclines to mercy, by which the sinner is so helped that he may return to justice.

The sixth and seventh beatitudes pertaining to the contemplative life are not found in the account of Luke, and more probably were not preached to the people but to the disciples.

While many philosophers were saying: beatitude is in the speculation of the truth, and were caring little about purity of heart; Jesus says: Blessed are the clean of heart, they shall see God, that is, they already receive in this life the understanding of

divine things or the contemplation of the mysteries of salvation
in intimate conversation with God, and in this way they will be
able to preach from the abundance of the heart. This beatitude of
cleanliness of heart, according to St. Augustine and St. Thomas,
corresponds to the gift of understanding, from which is had a
penetration of divine things; thus, living faith becomes penetrating,
it understands the mysteries and especially the superiority of the
ultimate end in respect to the other ends: how God is to be loved
above all things immensely surpasses the objects of concupiscence
and pride. This is the contemplation from which derives fruitful
preaching in the Apostles.

Next it is said: *Blessed are the peacemakers, for they shall
be called the children of God*; these are the true wise men, the
blessed, not because they are peacemakers in a human fashion, but
because they consider all things according to their relationship to
God, and for that reason they were not being troubled, but instead
they find, preserve, and communicate true peace to others who
were being troubled. Now this peace is the tranquility of order
which is possessed from the gift of wisdom, for this gift judges
about all things connaturally by referring to God, in this way it
is somewhat experimentally known that evil would not happen if
it were not permitted by God on account of a greater good. In this
manner peace is preserved, and those peacemakers reconcile men
who are divided amongst themselves. In this manner the great
shepherds or bishops are peacemakers (cf. II-II, q. 45).

Finally the eighth beatitude is the most perfect of all, for it
expresses perseverance in the others, notwithstanding unjust
vexations, namely: *Blessed are they that suffer persecution for
justice's sake, for theirs is the kingdom of heaven.* This merit arises
from all the virtues and gifts, especially from heroic patience in
persecutions, by which the soul is ultimately purified, such that
amidst torments themselves is found a superhuman happiness
[beatitude]. These sublime words were completely unheard-of,
and in them is shown a supernatural wisdom and abnegation.
Concerning these things, Chrysostom says: "He who seeks only
God's glory, does not fear to be confounded in the sight of men."

Theirs is the kingdom of heaven; this is the joy of contemplation and of union with God amidst persecutions themselves.

This is the loftiness of Christian perfection, described in the concrete and vividly; it immensely surpasses a merely human perfection about which the Greek wise men were speaking, just as grace surpasses nature. And these words illustrate the proposition in which is summarized the whole Sermon on the Mount, namely, *"Be you therefore perfect, as also your heavenly Father is perfect,"* that is to say, with a supernatural perfection, not only angelic, but divine, which is ordered to seeing God as He immediately sees Himself and to loving Him for eternity.

To this perfection especially priests ought to tend.

* * *

The correlation of the virtues and the gifts
can be better expressed in this way:

Grace — theological virtues	charity	the gift of wisdom	Blessed are the peacemakers
	faith	the gift of understanding	Blessed are the clean of heart
	hope	the gift of knowledge	Blessed are the clean of heart
cardinal virtues	prudence	the gift of counsel	Blessed are the merciful
	justice (religion)	the gift of piety	Blessed are the meek
	fortitude	the gift of fortitude	Blessed are they that hunger and thirst after justice
	temperance	the gift of fear	Blessed are the poor

The fruits of the Holy Ghost: charity, joy, peace, patience, benignity, goodness, longanimity, mildness, faith, modesty, continency, chastity (Gal. 5:22).

CHAPTER III

ON THE FALSE NOTIONS OF THE INTERIOR LIFE COMPARED WITH THE TRUE NOTION: AND ON THE TWO PRINCIPAL MEANS TO OBTAIN IT

Spiritual theology ought to unify in the practical order those things which are taught in St. Thomas' various tracts of theology.

State of the question: From whence exactly are born the false notions of Christian perfection, especially today? —Many Christians, although they believe in *the Redemption of mankind through Christ* in general, do not sufficiently think about their *own personal sanctification*, of their own individual salvation. — On the contrary, very many first Christians were considering attentively their own sanctification to be generously fulfilled.

Moreover today, under the influence of Naturalism, many men, even Christians, no longer see *the value of a modest, personal Christian life* and in practice they seem to think that the value of modern civilization surpasses the supernatural nobility of soul of the first Christians. On the contrary, the terrible regression of modern civilization arises from the fact that it is no longer profoundly Christian, as it ought to be.

Hence the principles concerning the value of the redemption must be inculcated in a practical manner, not only in general, but for the benefit of every single Christian, even the most modest, taken individually in order to move him to greater personal generosity.

St. Bernard, St. John of the Cross, St. Francis de Sales, and recently for the benefit of priests, Cardinal Mercier, in *The Interior Life, Call to Priestly Souls*, 1919, (p. 83-123), and many others, among whom is Canon Maurice Garrigou, my paternal great-uncle, who during the French Revolution exercised a fruitful priestly ministry in the city of Toulouse; wrote in different ways about this matter. I cite his principle writing on the interior life, published in *Revue d'Ascétique et de Mystique*, 1937, p. 124-140: "Considerations on the Interior Life."

On the false notions of the interior life. Certain persons view it as a state of spirituality in which the feeling of sensibility prevails; it is *sentimentalism* or a pretense in the sensibility of a love which does not exist, or does not sufficiently exist, in the spiritual will. Then effective charity is neglected, and only affective charity is considered, which is adulterated and confounded with sensible devotion. It is just like a fleeting flame from straw, to which succeeds spiritual sloth, from which the mind departs with difficulty. Hence, these persons erroneously suppose themselves to have an interior life which they do not have, but they simulate it before having it.

Others, on the contrary, suppose that the true interior life is something so lofty, that it is extraordinary, as a privilege reserved for a few and inaccessible for others; and thus they remain in some mechanical action of exercises in which they do not find life, which they consequently seek in external activity.

These two false conceptions err about the end to be sought and about the principle means, as will presently appear more clearly.

Other false notions of the interior life can be reduced to these two aforesaid ones. Cardinal Mercier describes them in this manner: Some reckon the interior life to be the privilege of a few, and inaccessible to others. Others despair of coming to it, on account of some sin of fragility, while the principle obstacle is not this fragility, but pride. — Others through inexperience confound imaginary perfection with the real and concrete perfection to which, according to the Gospel, they *here and now* ought to tend, in accordance with God's will. Others more or less think that perfection is connected with a special natural ability which they do not have. They do not consider that humility is the fundamental condition for the life of union, of which the principle is supernatural charity conferred upon all Christians by Baptism, and which is nourished by Holy Communion. — These persons all err both about the end to be attained and about the principle means to the end.

* * *

What exactly therefore is **the true notion of the interior life derived from its end and principle means?** — All the great spiritual authors reply: The interior life is *the life of intimate union or conversation with God, which is to be reached through perfect abnegation and constant recollection in which prayer continues.*

This doctrine, which is developed by St. Augustine, St. Ambrose, St. Bernard, St. Thomas, by the *Imitation of Christ,* by St. John of the Cross, by St. Francis de Sales, is based upon many texts of Sacred Scripture, especially on these words of St. Paul: "If you be risen with Christ (by Baptism), seek the things that are above, where Christ is sitting at the right hand of God; mind the things that are above, not the things that are upon the earth. *For you are dead: and your life is hid with Christ in God.* When Christ shall appear, who is your life, then you also shall appear with him in glory..." (Col. 3:1-4). — "But above all these things have charity, which is the bond of perfection" (*Ibid.* 3:14). That is: You are dead in respect to the life of sin, your new life is hidden, namely, it is the life of sanctifying grace, which with charity is the seed of glory.

Hence every just man, every soul in the state of grace ought to tend to the interior life thus conceived, so that finally he can say with St. Paul: *"And I live, now not I, but Christ liveth in me"* (Gal. 2:20). For the new life, which was infused into me through Baptism and is nourished by Communion, is the life of Christ, the Head of the mystical body, of which I am a member. And thus we ought to live more and more from this superior life so that *Christ lives more in us,* than we ourselves; so that through Him, and with Him, and in Him we think, will, suffer, and work, in such a way, namely, that His life is extended, and protracted in ours.

More briefly: "Our life is hid with Christ in God," who wills always to live more in us as in His members according to that which is written: "I am the true vine, you are the branches."

This is manifestly, according to the Gospel's Revelation, the true notion of the interior life from its goal, i.e. from the intimate union with God through Christ. Consult concerning this, the *Imitation of Christ* (bk. II, chap. 1), on the internal conversation with God, the explanation of the Lord's words (Jn. 14:13): "If any one love me, he will keep my word. And my Father will love him

and we will come to him and will make our abode with him," i.e.
the Father and the Son and the Holy Ghost, have been promised
at the same moment.

But practically, to avoid all illusion, it is appropriate *to
consider well the distance between the point* of departure [*teminus
a quo*] *and point* of arrival [*teminus ad quem*] *of the spiritual
ascent.*

We have enunciated the goal to be achieved, but between this
summit and the initial state of the beginning soul is a notable
distance; namely, as notes Fr. Maurice Garrigou: "We live, but we
ourselves live rather than Christ in us. Why? Because there often
prevails in us 'vanity, levity of mind, inconstancy, dissipation,
the bewitching of vanity obscuring good things' (Wis. 4:12), and
inordinate love of oneself, by which is impeded the progress of
charity towards God and neighbor. We often so live not internally
but externally, on the outer surface of the imagination and
sensibility; our soul flees itself, it is external to itself, and the lowest
depth of our soul remains unknown to us. On the contrary, one
ought to stay in this lowest depth where the Holy Trinity dwells.
This is necessary so that Christ's kingdom may be stabilized in
us, and so that He may live in us, as the true vine in the branches,
as the head in the members. This interior life, however, remains
to us as if it were another unknown region, while it might have
been entirely beneficial to us."

Now to reach this goal two means are altogether necessary,
namely, *abnegation* and *constant recollection* in which prayer
continues or conversation with God. In this way is expressed
(in terms intentionally sober) in a simple manner, that which
otherwise is called (in terms somewhat emphatic) the ascent to
union with God through the purgative way, in which abnegation
prevails, and the illuminative way, in which is kept constant
recollection with prayer quasi continuous.

However, these two means are to be attentively and practically
considered in the concrete according to the circumstances in which
each one is found.

"*Abnegation,*" according to St. Basil, "is like a separation
from our own will which is not in conformity with the divine will."

According to St. John of the Cross, abnegation is the mysterious death to all more or less inordinate inclinations. Out of this voluntary emptying arises the silence of the inordinate passions and tranquility of soul, quiet and peace, the foundation of the interior life. But it is an illusion, if we think that our immoderate passions are dead, when they are asleep. That which is expelled promptly returns; that which is extinguished is again enkindled. And thus one must be vigilant about spontaneous [*primo-primi*] movements so that they are not protracted. Abnegation of oneself is a voluntary death to the world, namely, to vanity, pride, one's more or less inordinate own judgement, and one's own impetuosity. This abnegation also prevents one from seeking complacency in his virtues, in his knowledge, so that he may remain humble and modest. Therefore this abnegation is that which St. Paul expresses, saying: *I die daily*, namely, to a lower life, so that I may receive a higher life. Now in this renunciation, dispossession or voluntary expropriation, *the soul becomes completely docile to the Holy Ghost*, because it is no longer moved by its own inordinate self-love. Then the seven gifts of the Holy Ghost are exercised more easily; before they were like a furled sail on a ship, now they are like *a sail not furled but extended* under the impulse of a favorable wind. Then the intellect follows the inclination of the renewed heart, because everyone judges according to their own inclination, and because a pure heart is inflamed with the love of God, this flame always ascends to God. In this way the soul, liberated from every impediment of self-love or of egoism, adheres with its heart to the most Sacred Heart of Jesus, "heart to heart," and then it is fully opened to inspirations of God, who, as it were, speaks spiritually with it through the inspirations of the seven gifts, which are in any just man. In this way "the Spirit himself giveth testimony to our spirit that we are the sons of God" (Rom. 8:16).

Abnegation taken in this way practically and concretely leads *to habitual recollection*, which is the second necessary means to union with God. Thus inconstant souls unhappily do not reach to this goal, who live one day in recollection, but not the following day, nay they become very exterior, such that they are deprived of great graces, and seem to never have understood that which the Psalmist says: "O taste, and see that the Lord is sweet" (Ps. 33:9).

This constant recollection is expressed by Christ the Lord when He says: "*We ought always to pray and not to faint*" (Lk. 18:1), namely, with the internal prayer of desire always ascending to God; it is like the soul's respiration, to breathe the actual grace which continually comes to us just as air comes to our breast for the renewal of blood in the lung. (An indifferent act is not possible in the individual case. Cf. St. Th. I-I, q. 18, a. 9.)

This is the true illuminative way, according as in this recollection, quasi continual prayer, and docility to the Holy Ghost continues.

Hence the author of the *Imitation* wonderfully says: "There are many who desire contemplation, but they endeavor not to practice those things that are needful thereunto." And just before: "Unless a man be set free from all creatures, he cannot wholly attend unto divine things. And therefore are there so few contemplatives, for that few can wholly withdraw themselves from things created and perishing. To obtain this, there is need of much grace, to elevate the soul, and carry it away above itself. And unless a man be lifted in spirit, and be freed from all creatures, and wholly united unto God, whatsoever he knoweth, and whatsoever he hath, is of small account. Far more noble is that learning which floweth from above, from the divine influence, than that which is painfully gotten by the wit of man" (bk. III, chap. 31 "Of the contempt of all creatures, in order to find out the Creator").

Indeed it is much more noble, and it is necessary that a priest can preach the divine word *from the abundance of the heart:* "A good man out of a good treasure bringeth forth good things" (Mt. 12:34). As it is said in the same place: This good treasure does not remain idle.

* * *

First Conclusion: Therefore perfect abnegation and continual recollection, which is maintained with the prayer of desire even in the external ministry, naturally leads the Christian soul, especially the priestly soul, to intimate union with God, namely, to true joy, nay to youth, to the unitive life of the perfect, which is a treasure out of which the priest brings forth good things. This intimate union, however, proceeds from a living faith enlightened by the gifts of the Holy Ghost and from a charity at the same time affective and effective. For in this way faith, enlightened by the gifts of understanding and wisdom, normally becomes penetrating and savoring, that is to say, it penetrates the mysteries of salvation and tastes them; in this way it disposes to a special act of charity, which is called an *infused act*, because it not only proceeds from infused charity, but also from a special inspiration. This infused act is nevertheless vital, free, meritorious, according as it docilely proceeds from the mind under a special inspiration of the Holy Ghost. In this way, in the proper sense, "the Holy Ghost giveth testimony to our spirit that we are the sons of God." He gives this testimony through the infused filial affection which He awakens in us by the gift of piety. This intimate union with God is *in the normal way to sanctity*, because it proceeds connaturally from the three theological virtues and from the gifts of the Holy Ghost, which are in any just man and which are augmented as infused habits with charity, which always ought to grow even unto death.

Hence, Christ's priest ought to aspire humbly, but at the same time confidently and ardently, to this intimate union with God and Jesus Christ, in order that he may be united in this way with Christ the sovereign Priest and may be able to nourish the souls of his flock. Now humility and confidence ought to be united in every prayer. Otherwise the priest will not be another Christ.

This intimate union is indeed *eminent*, but not something *extraordinary* by right [*de jure*], in this it differs from the properly extraordinary graces such as prophecy, the knowledge of the secrets of the heart, stigmatism, the gift of tongues, etc.

In this state of unitive life are verified in a different manner the words of St. Paul: "I bow my knees to the Father of our Lord Jesus Christ... that he would grant you, according to the riches of his glory, to be strengthened by his Spirit with might unto the inward man; that Christ may dwell by faith in your hearts, that, being rooted and founded in charity, you may be able to comprehend, with all the saints, what is the breadth and length and height and depth; to know also the charity of Christ, which surpasseth all knowledge, that you may be filled unto all the fullness of God" (Eph. 3:14-19).

"That is," says St. Thomas, "that you might enjoy a perfect participation in all God's gifts. In other words, that you might possess the fullness of virtues here, and beatitude in the next life— charity accomplishes just that."

This does not mean, however, that in the unitive life there are no longer *crosses*, on the contrary, then the value of the cross is understood more, nay the *love of the cross* or of Christ crucified is possessed, with the desire of participating in His sorrowful life according to that passage of St. Paul: "Now I rejoice in my sufferings for you and fill up those things that are wanting of the sufferings of Christ, in my flesh, for his body, which is the church" (Col. 1:24). For in this way Christ, the head of the mystical body, raises up in some of His members a reparative life, for saving others. Just as the Highest Cause gives the dignity of causality to creatures, so Christ the Redeemer gives to some of His members a reparative life. In other words, these just men repair in Christ, through Christ and with Christ, so that there may be applied to them and to others the merits of the Passion, which in themselves are of infinite value and therefore superabundant. Nothing is lacking in these merits, only their full application is lacking in us and in the sinners to be redeemed.

Second Conclusion: It must be feared that we insufficiently respond to this calling of Christ. For this calling to intimate union with God corresponds for the priest not only to a counsel, but even to a precept or an obligation of tending to the perfection of charity. And not only, as we have said, is there a *general obligation* based upon the supreme precept of love of God and of neighbor, but a *special obligation* founded upon the priestly ordination and upon the priestly functions. Consequently, not to respond to this calling is a grave enough matter. For Christ calls His priests to an intimate union with Himself. He calls in various ways: exteriorly through the Gospel, through preaching in spiritual exercises; He calls interiorly in our heart; He calls frequently, and many times. If the priest does not respond to this calling, if he does not come, does not hear, but even goes backward, *it must be feared that Christ will no more call in the same manner, in the same way "He knocks at the gate of our heart."*[1] Then the proximately sufficient graces, which the soul resists, become rarer and perhaps remain only remotely sufficient graces to intimate union with God, from the fact that the priest "did not know the time of the Lord's visitation." But then the priest ought to say to himself: Nevertheless I am a priest and souls are in need of my ministry; as Augustine says, *"God does not command impossible things, but by commanding He bids us to do what we can and to ask for what we cannot do."* Therefore it must be implored with humility, confidence, perseverance, and Christ will again hear me, so that I may be able to fruitfully work in His vineyard. It is also said for my sake: *"Come to me all you that labor and are burdened, and I will refresh you."*

And then the priest ought to continue the ascent until he arrives at the summit, to which he was called on the day of his ordination; and this especially is necessary on account of the great need of the souls of his flock, nor ought he to interrupt the journey before he arrives at the goal.

This doctrine is based upon the Gospel, upon the Epistles of St. Paul, in that which St. Augustine, St. Thomas, St. John of the Cross and St. Francis de Sales afterwards taught concerning the loftiness of the supreme precept; concerning the charity of the wayfarer, which always ought to grow until death; concerning the seven gifts connected with charity, which are normally increased with it as infused habits.

Likewise this is based upon the fact that, in order that the priest may preach from the abundance of the heart, it is required that he have a living faith illumined by the gifts of the Holy Ghost, and both an affective and effective charity, which is truly communicative for the salvation of souls.

More briefly: **in order that the priest truly be another Christ**, in his soul ought to be the ardor of charity (in other

---

1 Apoc. 3:20: "Behold, I stand at the gate and knock: if any man shall hear my voice, and open to me the door, I will come in to him, and will sup with him, and he with me."

words, a zeal for God's glory and the salvation of souls) which is
not without, as it were, a continuous colloquy with Christ about
the ministry to be fulfilled in His name. — This is not merely
probable, but is certain.

For the completion of those things which we have said about
perfect abnegation and recollection in order that the priest may
arrive at perfection, it ought to be treated *concerning the connection*
of the virtues and *concerning the progressive purification of the*
virtues in respect to obtaining this perfection. In this the harmony
will more clearly appear between the doctrine of St. Thomas about
the virtues and gifts of the Holy Ghost and the doctrine of the
great spiritual authors such as St. John of the Cross, St. Francis
de Sales and others.

CHAPTER IV

ON THE CONNECTION OF THE VIRTUES FOR OBTAINING PRIESTLY PERFECTION

I. — On the connection of the virtues inasmuch as it is the fruit of the Holy Ghost

In our time, after so great disturbances of peoples, many speak about a new world, of a new order; but they do not sufficiently give heed to that thing which the Church often says, that there ought to be a connection between tradition and progress, because the present time cannot produce a worthy and fruitful future, unless it is fertilized by that which is better in the past. Old things are increased by new things, otherwise the new time is without foundation and passes without any fruit; if it despises the past, it will be despised after useless attempts.

As has often been said, in every living organism there ought to be an *assimilative power of new nourishment, and a conservative power*, and equilibrium between them; if there is no new assimilation death ensues, and if a conservation of assimilated nourishment is lacking, death also ensues through the complete loss of resources.

Likewise, in order that a vehicle may go forward correctly, there ought to be a motor power and also a brake in case of a dangerous descent.

So *in the Church* and in every society there ought to be an equilibrium between the *progressive power* and the *conservative power*; if there is not any progress, there is the immobility of death, as in the schismatic Eastern churches; and if there is not a conservative tradition, there is the instability of perpetual variation, as in liberal Protestantism, and in Socialism leading to materialistic Communist and Atheism; then the descent without any brake becomes most dangerous.

For keeping the equilibrium of powers, either in individual life or in collective life, *natural dynamism does not suffice* for us Christians, e.g. democratic aspirations: these aspirations can indeed at some time help against dictatorship or totalitarianism, but most evidently they do not suffice without Christian traditions for keeping the aforesaid equilibrium.

On the contrary, this equilibrium is established by the Holy Ghost *through the connection of the virtues*, concerning which I now wish to speak, as it were, concerning the precious fruit of the Holy Ghost (Gal. 5:22).

Firstly, it especially ought to be recalled to memory that *sins* are not connected. As notes St. Thomas (I-II, q. 73, a. 1), although all *mortal sins* concur in their aversion from God, and thus one cannot be remitted without the other, nevertheless *they are not connected*; nay they are often opposed to each other, such as avarice and prodigality, such as laziness and rashness. For that reason, evils are opposed to each other and finally mutually destroy themselves.

On the contrary, the intention of all the virtues tend to the same thing, and on account of this, all the virtues, at least in the firm state of the virtue, are connected to each other in prudence and charity.

Imperfect virtues, or if in the state of an easily movable disposition, *are indeed not connected*, and are of three kinds:

a) A natural inclination from one's temperament to fortitude is often without an inclination to kindness.

b) Likewise, the acquired disposition to fortitude in a soldier who fights, not out of a love of virtue but out of a desire for glory, is often together with voluptuousness, and sometimes this voluptuousness impedes this soldier to fulfill his duty to serve as a soldier.

c) Even true virtues which are only developing, still in the state of an easily movable disposition, are not yet connected; for example, someone may have an incipient justice without chastity.

d) Nay, *as long as the soul remains in the state of mortal sin, its acquired virtues*, which are developing, *are not connected*; because this soul is turned away from the ultimate end and hence is weak in keeping even ordinary natural obligations, e. g. in matters of justice, fortitude, patience, chastity, etc.

Secondly, by opposition, *the Holy Ghost having come* into the soul by charity, which is poured out in our hearts, the *true* acquired *virtues*, which were developing in it, are made firm, and if they are sufficiently firm, solid, stable, *they are connected*. All the more *the infused virtues* are connected with charity, as properties of sanctifying grace (I-II, q. 65, a .1 and 2).

In this way, in the just man is verified, in the acquired virtues, that which was being said by Aristotle, namely, *true prudence* (which is altogether distinct from shrewdness, from utilitarianism and opportunism) *is not able to be without the moral virtues, nor the latter without prudence, which directs them all*; in this manner prudence is truly the "driver of the virtues," the "correct notion of acting [*recta ratio agibilium*]" (Ethics, bk. 6, last chap.).

The principle reason of this connection is that "*what type each person is according to his affection, that kind of end seems agreeable to him*"; an ambitious man judges that which favors ambition to be suitable, and a modest man that which is conformed to modesty.

More briefly: *anyone whom you please judges according to his inclinations* of will and of sensibility. And therefore, if these inclinations are not rectified through the virtues, the practical judgment will not be correct, it will sometimes be apparently prudent on account of some sharp sightedness, experience or astuteness, but it will not be truly prudent. For there will be in him a defect either of justice, or of patience, or of temperance, or of kindness, or of simplicity, or perhaps it will be duplicity, together sometimes with precipitation, and sometimes with laziness.

Hence, the Holy Ghost coming into the soul establishes through charity and Christian prudence the connection of the infused virtues and also of the acquired virtues, if it will have been sufficiently exercised for their acquisition. In this way consequently all the virtues are increased at the same time, says St. Thomas, "just as five fingers of the hand" (I-II, q. 66, a. 2).

Moreover the Holy Ghost makes the connection of the virtues and of the gifts, for, as St. Thomas shows (I-II, q. 68, a. 5), the seven gifts are connected with charity, just as the Holy Ghost and the holy sevenfold [gifts] are given to us with charity. And this is verified therefore in any just man, but according to the various degrees of charity. This harmony is marvelous, especially in those who go forth to perfection. In this way, *chastity* amidst temptations is helped *by the gift of fear*: "Pierce, O Lord, my flesh with thy fear"; *fortitude* amidst adversities is helped *by the gift of fortitude*, especially in the martyrs; *justice* towards God, namely, religion which renders to God the worship which is due to Him, is helped, especially in the time of involuntary aridity, *by the gift of piety*, from which arises a filial affection towards God. *Prudence* in very complex affairs, and in respect to unforeseeable matters, is helped *by the gift of counsel. Faith* is helped *by the gift of understanding*, in such a way that it penetrates the mysteries of salvation. *Hope*, in like manner, is helped against presumption *by the gift of fear*, and it is animated by the illumination *of the gift of knowledge* about the vanity of created things, and the gravity of sin; in this way, through hope, we more vividly desire God [Who is] to be possessed and His grace. — Finally, *charity* is helped *by the gift of wisdom*, by which we consider all things in God, the supreme cause and ultimate end; in this way we see that all good things come forth from Him, and that evil does not happen unless it is permitted by Providence for a higher good, which we sufficiently perceive in part so that we may cooperate towards its realization. *Peace* arises from this, and for that reason the beatitude of the peacemakers corresponds, according to Augustine, to the gift of wisdom.

Nevertheless since the intellectual gifts are simultaneously speculative and practical, in certain just men they appear more under a contemplative form, and in others under a practical form, more directly ordained to action, as in St. Vincent de Paul.

Thirdly, this wonderful harmony, or connection of the virtues and gifts, is the fruit of the Holy Ghost. For it is said to the Galatians (5:22-23): "The fruit of the Spirit is charity, joy, peace, patience, benignity, goodness, longanimity, mildness, faith, modesty, continency, chastity," which are opposed to the works of the flesh, e.g. lust and dissentions.

This wonderful harmony appeared especially *in Jesus Christ*, as in Him were joined and in an intimate manner *even the virtues most distant from each other*, which can only be united by God in a holy soul. For the Lord Jesus had all the virtues, even the most diverse, in a heroic degree. In Him are wonderfully conciliated the most ardent *charity towards God* and an immense *mercy towards all sinners*; in Him are united a *holy love of truth and justice* and the *greatest compassion towards the erring*, towards His very own torturers, for whom He prays at the moment of crucifixion, such that the words of the Psalmist are verified in Him: "Mercy and truth have met each other: justice and peace have kissed" (Ps. 84:11).

Likewise, in Him are intimately united a *profound humility*, by which He accepts all humiliations for us, and the *greatest dignity* or magnanimity, e.g. in His responses to Pilate and to Caiphas. Similarly, in Him are united the *greatest fortitude* in martyrdom and the *greatest mildness* in the same moment of crucifixion. Finally, He had at the same time the *highest wisdom* together with contemplation, and perfect *prudence* which was descending *to the lowest* particular affairs.

This sublime harmony and perseverance of heroic virtues in Christ is a moral miracle, as Apologetics shows, a miracle without doubt confirming Christ's testimony of his divine filiation.

Something similar, in a lesser degree, is found in the true martyrs, and according of St. Thomas (Quodlibet 4, a. 9) and Benedict XIV (*De servorum Dei beatific., bk. 3, c. 21) true martyrs are distinguished from the false ones especially through the connection of virtues.* For according to the example of the Lord and St. Stephen, true martyrs are at the same time strong and humble, and also mild, for they pray for their persecutors. False martyrs do not do this, in whom fanaticism is a certain blind obstinacy which shuns discussion, and excludes wisdom, prudence, modesty, humility and mildness. As Apologetics shows, God's own effect appears in the constancy of the martyrs, especially on account of the connection of the most diverse virtues, which can only be joined together by God, just as infinite Justice and infinite Mercy are united in the Deity's eminence.

Conclusion: In the present time it is to be demanded, therefore, that men do penance for their sins, for the works of the flesh, which are "luxury, service of (modern) idols, enmities, contentions, emulations, wraths, quarrels, dissentions, sects, envies."

It must be prayed that the Holy Ghost impart to us His fruits, which are "charity, joy, peace, patience, benignity, goodness, longanimity, mildness, faith, modesty, continency, chastity." — It must be besought and accomplished daily *in order that we may attain to the connection of virtues in charity*, "which is patient, is kind,...which beareth all things, believeth all things, hopeth all things, endureth all things."

Only in this way, in our individual life and in the collective life of the religious Orders and of the Church, is *the conservative force and the progressive force* conciliated, and in this way that which is *in the past* will be conserved, so that a worthy and fruitful *future* might be prepared, so that it may truly be a *certain beginning of eternal life.*

II. — Applications of the doctrine "of the connection of the virtues" to priestly perfection.

"The Spirit of truth will teach you all truth" (Jn. 16:13), but "try the spirits if they be of God" (1 Jn. 4:1).

I would now like to apply the doctrine of the connection of the virtues and gifts in order to better examine priestly and religious perfection.

At the present time, a renewal of the interior life must be demanded, for which two qualities are required: *unity of the mind* for the intellect to judge correctly in so great a complexity about preserving tradition and about making progress; moreover *a living flame of charity* for the heart is required, in order that it be not only an affective, but also an effective and fruitful charity.

But every false mystic says in his presumption, that he gives this unity of mind and ardor of love. Even the mystic of communism [i.e. one initiated into its hidden 'mysteries'], although he is materialistic and atheistic, says that he furnishes these two qualities, but he leads to tyranny and universal servitude.

Nor suffice for the finding of these two qualities, as it is clear, aspirations which little by little, in place of true faith, hope and love of God, substitute faith and hope in humanity together with merely theoretical love of humanity. These are the large ideas having fallen down into insanity, "the great ideas have become follies," as says Chesterton.

In order that unity of mind for the intellect and love of God and neighbor in the heart be in us, the *connection of the virtues* is required, namely, of true faith, hope, and charity, of the moral virtues and gifts.

This connection is greatly opposed to romantic sentimentalism, which does not care about the virtues, and this connection greatly helps the examination of conscience and true spiritual progress.

Without this connection, a priest is not able to unite all the qualities necessary for himself, and which are today urgently necessary.

Firstly, in the priest there ought to be both a *conservation* of the true Christian tradition and a *progress* in true charity towards the neighbor, by which is promoted a greater distributive and social justice for removing the excessive inequality of conditions.

For this, the *spirit of* liturgical *prayer* helps greatly, especially in the celebration of the Mass, and true *Eucharistic worship*. For the Eucharist contains at the same time *that which was better in the past*, namely, Christ's Passion, of which it is the memorial and application, and *that which will be better in the future*, namely, the progress of charity so that it is the beginning of eternal life. It does not suffice to know historically what Christ said of old, what ought to be considered is how He now influences the life of the Church. Now, the Eucharist contains "Christ always living to make intercession for us," Christ who actually offers the Masses which are celebrated daily. Hence, the living Eucharistic worship best conciliates that which was better in the past and that which will be better in the future, in the way to eternal life.

Secondly, in this way also *the interior life and the external apostolate* are united in the priestly life. Out of the neglect of prayer the apostolate becomes excessively exterior, sterile, no longer living; because it is separated from the living fountain, it becomes somewhat "mechanical." In order that it be living and fruitful it ought to proceed "from the abundance of the heart."

Now, in order that the interior life may in this way become "the soul of the apostolate," progressive abnegation and habitual recollection are required, which lead to a living faith enlightened by the gifts of understanding and wisdom, to the spirit of prayer or filial piety towards God, to operating charity. Only in this way does the priest truly become the salt of the earth and the light of the world.

Thirdly, he also ought to unite in himself a *firm faith* without any complacency for the error, and a *great compassion* towards those erring. He would decline from a firm faith through liberalism, which leads to indifferentism; and from compassion through rigorism, e.g. of the Jansenists. Hence his life ought to be like a pinnacle between and above these two deviations opposed to each other. Now this cannot occur without the connection of the virtues in an already elevated degree; which is perhaps not said enough at the time of discussions about liberalism.

Fourthly, the priest also ought to unite a *prudence* attentive to particular things and *simplicity*: "the wisdom [*prudentia*] of a serpent and the simplicity of a dove." He would recede from simplicity and fall into duplicity by declining to utilitarianism, to opportunism, which leads to craftiness. And on the other hand, he would withdraw from true prudence if his simplicity were excessively naïve, if he were not to see the evil to be avoided where it is truly found, nor discern the snares of evil men, who abuse the simplicity of the good. Hence is required, especially in difficult times, the connection of a lofty prudence without utilitarianism, and of a lofty simplicity without naiveté. Now this is impossible without the connection of the virtues and also of the gifts.

Fifthly, the priest also ought to unite the *firmness* of justice and fortitude with *mildness*. In other words, his firmness ought to be without rigidity, for that reason he ought to possess, beyond commutative justice, distributive and social justice and also *equity,* or *epikeia*, which is more attentive to the spirit of the law than to its letter, especially where "the highest right would be the greatest injury [*summum jus esset summa injuria*]." This must be particularly said in our time in which equity is so rare. — On the other hand, the priest's mildness ought not to decline to inept weakness and indulgence towards the evil men, from which the good would suffer on account of the audacity of the evil men. — For this also the connection of the virtues is required in an elevated degree.

Sixthly, the priest, moreover, ought to unite *true humility* with *dignity* or magnanimity, always tending to great things. These two virtues are not contrary, but complementary, and mutually help each other, just as two arches of the same ogive which support a building. In this way magnanimity hinders humility from declining to pusillanimity, and humility hinders magnanimity from degenerating into pride and ambition. Pride is the inordinate love of one's own excellence, magnanimity moderately tends to great things worthy of great honor, without the inordinate desire of honor; rather it despises honors in comparison to the great thing to which it tends strongly and sweetly.

Finally the priest ought to have absolute and perfect *chastity*, but *without insensibility of the heart*, because he ought to have compassion for the afflicted and to sympathize with them.

All these things demand the connection of the virtues in an already eminent degree. This is most evident. May this, with the Holy Ghost assisting, be accomplished in us. To this end one must pray. "Ask and you shall receive." This must be petitioned in the name of the Lord Jesus.

In practice, one must especially insist upon the intimate union of *humble obedience* and *fraternal charity*. For as St. Francis de Sales says, humble obedience, which keeps the best traditions, is like a deeper *root* of a tree, which always penetrates more into the ground for drawing its juices, while fraternal charity is like a *higher* and more fruitful *branch*, which is always more elevated and fructifies. There is a connection of these two parts of the tree, just as of these two virtues in the just soul.

If in the tree the deeper root and higher branch exercise their functions well, this tree is very good. Likewise, if in some soul, or even in some community, humble obedience and fraternal charity advance, this soul or this community is good, and if something is lacking as to prudence or energy, God then supplies through the gifts of counsel and fortitude.

This doctrine is full of consolation. While sins, happily, are not connected but frequently contrary to each other, the virtues are connected, and also the gifts, in charity; in this way there cannot be, e.g. through Communion or from the work of the one working, an increase of charity, without there being at the same time an increase of the other infused virtues and of the seven gifts; "they grow at the same time just as the five fingers on a child's hand," or just as the diverse organs of the same organism.

Conclusion: In this way, little by little, *through the connection* and increase *of the virtues* both acquired and infused, the *priest's spiritual physiognomy* is constituted, such that he may truly correspond to his lofty vocation. This is evident in the life of holy priests and religious, especially in the life of the founders of Orders.

In this way, notwithstanding great difficulties and sorrows, is kept, I would not say optimism, because natural optimism from one's temperament would not suffice; nor conventional optimism, which remains external, superficial; but *is kept something better than optimism*, namely, *confidence in God*, which is a strengthened infused hope, and *true charity* simultaneously affective and effective towards all, particularly towards helping the poor and the unfortunate.

In this way are obtained from the Holy Ghost, through humble, pious and persevering prayer, *two qualities of mind so necessary*, namely, *unity of spirit* for judging rightly in so great complexity, according to the Spirit of God and not merely according to the spirit of nature, and a *living flame of love* in the one advancing. In this manner the *spirit of tradition* and the *spirit of true progress* are best reconciled, so that the present time, fertilized by the past, may produce a fruitful future, which may truly be in us a prelude of eternal life.

CHAPTER V

ON THE NECESSARY PURIFICATION OF VIRTUES FOR CHRISTIAN PERFECTION

After consideration of the connection of the virtues with respect to priestly perfection, it is opportune to treat about the progressive purification of the virtues.

State of the question: St. John of the Cross speaks about this at length, and he begins by speaking in *The Dark Night* (bk. 1), *on the defects of beginners*: which are especially a certain *spiritual gluttony*, namely, an immoderate desire for sensible consolation (sentimentalism as it is called today), and a certain unconscious, secret *spiritual pride*, from which defects follow, in the time of aridity, *spiritual sloth* or laziness. — That is, little by little the capital sins appear again, but with respect to matters of piety. And this is a sign that the virtues are not sufficiently purified from the admixture of self-love, they are not therefore strong enough. And so a serious purification is required. — But St. John of the Cross does not speak about the subsequent defects in the ministry of souls.

And in order that I may speak more practically for our time, I briefly expose the defects of young priests and religious, relative to their external activity, according as they are observed without any exaggeration, nay, with great benevolence by their many directors, under the title "on the preparation for the ministry, for young priests."

On the defects of young priests, even after a good formation. — Their preparation is a grave obligation of conscience for Superiors, so that the young priests be truly prepared for contact with the real world, and from contact with it they do not lose in part their interior life shortly after priestly ordination, while on the contrary they ought to be perfected in the world, for the purpose of truly laboring for the salvation of souls.

I will relate that which the Superior General of some Congregation, a very good and experienced man, wrote to me.

The difficulties to be overcome must be attentively observed. There is a great difference between the life of recollection of a seminary or of a monastery and the public life of the ministry.

And often young priests and religious, although very much given to study and truly pious, are in regard to the ministry truly and exceedingly naïve; they are in the strict sense *immature,* and consequently it must really be feared that the grave dangers of the life of the ministry will overcome their strength and produce a sad deviation.

For generally young priests, so far as they are young, are not prudent; they indeed have infused prudence as they are in the state of grace, but often acquired prudence is lacking in them, or it is only in initial development. Consequently the young priest, when he is good, is rather inclined *to indiscreet zeal,* he has excessive confidence in himself, but often unconsciously, and he can also be inclined to a secret sensuality which he confuses in his protestations with the pure desire of accomplishing good.

Nay, sometimes the young priest *reckons he already knows the spiritual ways of the Lord,* and through secret spiritual pride thinks he can lead souls to high perfection. Then the danger is more serious, because then the young priest is not doubtful about himself, but brings forward opinions with great security, and trusts excessively in himself; and he will see the mistakes committed by himself when perhaps it will be too late.

What follows? — The indiscreet zeal and satisfactions of the first ministry, which always come, impel the young priest *totally* to the ministry and he ardently says: "Give me souls, O Lord." Then, gradually, *he considers the time of prayer*, of study and of recollection, *as if it were lost time,* and it is easy to foresee what follows. His ministry is sterile; it ought to sanctify him and sanctify the faithful, and it rather impedes sanctification.

But what is more: the young priest is at the age in which is greatly felt *the desire of loving and of receiving love.* The saints, however, know their own weakness; they do not trust in themselves, but they perform that which obedience determines. Young priests generally are not so, they rather are reckless, they despise danger, they trust in themselves, "I am sure of myself," and then for this reason one must grieve.

And therefore they stand in need of a special preparation for the reality of life. One must absolutely insist upon the *necessity of the true interior life*, so that thereafter the priest may be able *to give* and *not to lose* in the ministry.

One ought to say in particular, and often, that the external ministry does not take the place of prayer, because in the ministry it is necessary *to give*, but we cannot *always give*; one must also *receive* from God, and in prayer light and love and fortitude are received.

Also are to be noted the *dangers of preaching, of the ministry of confession and of direction*, of visitations which might occur outside of obedience, and also of direction through secret letters about matters pertaining to conscience. Moreover, the young imprudent priest insensibly, little by little, lets go of the true and holy liberty of spirit, union with Jesus Christ, and wastes much time in useless matters or in affections which seem spiritual and do not help for true spiritual progress, neither on the part of the director, nor on the part of the person who is directed.

On account of these various dangers, in various Orders and Congregations the young priests are firstly occupied in the *internal* ministry of the Monastery itself, e.g. to take care of the lay brothers, and but only little by little and slowly are they applied to the *external* ministry. Moreover, they remain in some way under the charge of a more serious Father, who with wisdom and benevolence leads them to true maturity and complete priestly formation. By the judgment of the Major Superiors, this practical problem is of great importance for the true formation of the priestly conscience. In spiritual exercises, preachers and confessors ought to treat of this matter strongly and sweetly.

From these facts it is evident that in the young priests there is still required a great purification and strengthening of the virtues, which remain very imperfect and weak on account of the admixture of inordinate self-love, inasmuch as the soul, in seeking God, still very much seeks itself or its own satisfaction. This was not yet appearing at the time of the novitiate or seminary, but it clearly appears at the beginning of the ministry, with the natural activity not sufficiently sanctified and ordered to God. Hence some say: "The novices appear to be saints, but they are not; the young priests do neither appear to be saints, nor are they; and if they do not advance, they become empty and sterile in their apostolate."

On the necessary purification of virtues for Christian perfection. — St. Thomas spoke of this question by treating about the purged virtues and about the virtues of the purged soul (I-II, q. 61, a. 5), and St. John of the Cross discussed at length about both the active and the passive purification of the senses and of the spirit, particularly in *The Dark Night*.

This *purification* is now theologically explained as *the more and more any virtue, both acquired and infused, is exercised on account of its formal motive* and not particularly on account of an adjoined inferior motive. In this way any virtue is purified from all admixtures by which it is more or less adulterated. In this way humility is freed from all pusillanimity and false humility; religion and piety from all sentimentalism and spiritual gluttony; fortitude from all temerity, an excessive confidence in oneself; kindness from all weakness and excessive indulgence; prudence, not only from all imprudence and negligence, but also from all utilitarianism and opportunism. In this way the soul finds equilibrium and harmony, even between the above deviations opposed to each other, e.g. rigorism and liberalism, and in this way are reconciled a most firm faith against errors, and a great charity towards the erring.

It is clear that any virtue, by the very fact that it is specified by its proper object and its own formal motive, is so much the more purified, the more it attains this formal object without admixed imperfection. This ought to be attentively observed in the causes of beatification, so that the heroicity of the diverse virtues may be more apparent, and their quasi spirit may show itself to be above the quasi mechanically ordered external practice.

Just as gold is purified in a furnace from its dross, so also are the virtues purified, and this is said many times in Sacred Scripture. *"As gold is tried by fire in the furnace: so the Lord trieth the hearts"* (Prov. 17:7); *"The trial of your faith, much more precious than gold, which is tried by the fire"* (1 Peter 1:7). For in this way, little by little, faith believes solely on account of God's authority; hope trusts solely on account of the assisting Omnipotence; and charity loves God solely on account of His infinitely loveable goodness, without the inordinate desire for one's own consolation. Likewise, Jesus says: "*I am the true vine: and my Father is the husbandman. Every branch in me that beareth not fruit, he will take away: and every one that beareth fruit, he will purge it, that it may bring forth more fruit*" (John 15:1). In this text is treated about the passive purification which comes from God Himself, which is not chosen by us as the mortification which everyone ought to perform: e.g. "If thy right eye scandalize thee, pluck it out and cast it from thee" (Matt. 5:29).

This ought to be considered according to the principle virtues one by one, by ascending from the lower to the higher ones, and by noting how the gifts of the Holy Ghost help the virtues in this progressive purification. In this way it will be more apparent how in the life of God's servants, the heroicity of the virtues ought to be described by considering the formal object of each virtue and then their connection.

Temperance, and particularly chastity, is specified by the special "perfective" good [*bonum honestum*], *according to the moderation of the passions of the concupiscible appetite*. This moderation comes about according to right natural reason and acquired prudence, if it be treated about acquired chastity; however it comes about according to reason enlightened by faith and infused prudence, if it be treated about infused chastity.

Consequently, infused chastity is specified by a higher formal object than acquired chastity, and the latter is related as a disposition to the other, in some way as in a lute player the agility of the hands is to the art, which is in the practical intellect. In this way acquired chastity gives the extrinsic facility for the exercise of infused chastity.

In order that chastity be purified from all admixed imperfection, not only must the soul be freed from all sensuality more or less inordinate, from suspicious friendship, but even from insensibility of the heart, which appears to be a virtue and is not: it is opposed to due compassion.

Likewise, acquired *mildness* and infused mildness are purified, not only when the soul is freed from all anger, but from inept weakness and indulgence, which would be a false mildness.

In the same way, *humility,* which subjects us before the divine Majesty, ought to remove not only pride, but also false humility, which would be a hidden pusillanimity. And in this way humility and magnanimity are reconciled, which reasonably and in a Christian way tend to great things according to God's will; and more and more they show themselves to be complementary virtues, which mutually help each other just as two arches of some pointed arch which supports a building. The more every single thing is purified, the more it attains its formal object.

Fortitude, in like manner, is specified by a particular "perfective" good as it is the virtue moderating the movements of the soul concerning all frightful things whatsoever. In this way there is firmness of soul for not departing from right reason in withstanding and repelling these very difficult adversities. Acquired fortitude is regulated by the dictate of right reason, infused fortitude by the dictate of right reason enlightened by faith or by infused prudence.

And therefore not only one ought to put away inordinate, irrational and non-Christian fear, e.g. in the moment of persecution; not only must pusillanimity and cowardice be avoided; but also fortitude ought to be freed from all admixture of false fortitude, namely, from all temerity, obstinacy, harshness of fanaticism, from all rigorism, which would be against the virtue of mildness.

In this way fortitude is progressively purified as the formal motive of acquired fortitude, and the higher formal motive of infused fortitude stands out more and more above the opposed deviations of pusillanimity and temerity. In this matter, infused fortitude is often helped by the gift of fortitude, under whose inspiration the Christian arrives at the end of the difficult work begun, with confidence of evading all dangers. In such a way this gift altogether excludes inordinate fear, and surpasses infused fortitude, just as it itself surpasses acquired fortitude; nevertheless they are exercised in a unified manner, just as in music the agility of the hands, the skill in the practical intellect and the musical inspiration are exercised at the same time.

Justice, which renders to everyone his due, is specified by the keeping of another's right. That is to say, its formal object is the accepted right in exchange for something just or equivalently due to the other, according to the dictate either of reason alone (if it is treated of acquired justice) or of reason enlightened by faith (if it is treated of infused justice).

But it does not suffice to keep *commutative justice*; *distributive justice* must also be kept, particularly by him who, as father in a family or superior in a community, ought to correctly distribute useful goods, rewards, and burdens to diverse members of the family or community according to the dictate of both acquired and infused prudence.

Legal justice must also be kept, which prepares and determines just prescriptions or laws for the common good and keeps watch with regard to their observance.

Also *equity* or *epikeia* must be exercised, which considers not only the letter of the law but its spirit, according to the intention of the legislator, in order to avoid juridical formalism or excessive rigor, or the highest right which would be the greatest injury. Equity of the natural order already is a great virtue; *a fortiori* Christian equity commanded by charity is an even greater virtue.

Thus there are four species of justice, already noted by Aristotle in the natural order, and to be exercised according to the Christian spirit, precisely so that all species of injustice are removed, and justice itself is purified from formalism and juridical rigorism contrary to equity and charity, and from all inordinate desire of political faction.

Prudence in the same manner must be purified from all admixed disorder. It is the driver of the virtues, the right reason of acting: the already in fact acquired prudence which gives the dictate of right reason, and the higher infused prudence which gives the dictate of right reason illuminated by faith and helped by the gift of counsel.

This virtue, as was said above, is not able to be firm or in the state of a difficultly moveable virtue without the other moral virtues, because everyone judges practically according to his own inclination of will and sensibility. If this inclination is not rectified, the practical judgment is not correct, and it is not e.g. in accordance with justice; in accordance with patience; in accordance with mildness; in accordance with temperance; in accordance with humility; and in accordance with simplicity.

Hence, prudence not only ought to remove all imprudence (either from negligence, or from precipitation and impulse), but it ought to be purified, especially in the priest, from all utilitarianism and opportunism, which is not inspired by a love of virtue, but by the desire for one's own convenience or by an inordinate love of one's own family, or nation, or political faction. A higher purification of this virtue is especially required in Superiors, who ought to direct others correctly and in a Christian manner.

Religion, similarly, is the virtue which renders to God the worship of *latria* due to Him on account of His supreme excellence of Creator and Lord. Religion of the natural order is regulated only by right reason; infused religion, by faith through the medium of Christian prudence and the higher gift of piety, is regulated by the special inspiration of the Holy Ghost, by which we consider God not only as Creator but also as Father.

Religion, therefore, not only ought to remove irreligion, spiritual sloth or laziness, but also superstition; and ought to be purified from all sentimentalism, or the immoderate desire for sensible consolation in prayer; for this desire proceeds not from the love of God and true religion, but from egoism, according to which the soul does not seek God, but itself in matters of piety. — Now this purification, in order that it be perfect, not only ought to be active, from our own industry, but also passive, as is very well explained by St. John of the Cross in *The Dark Night* (bks. 1 and 2). One must specially insist upon this to show that this passive purification is in the normal way to sanctity, especially for the priest.

In this place, St. John of the Cross shows the necessity of this purification. Namely, in beginners, as it was said, there often is *spiritual gluttony*, or the immoderate desire for sensible consolation in prayer; *vanity* or *spiritual pride*, with the despising of others; and finally, when sensible consolation is lacking for a long time, come *spiritual sloth*, laziness, spiritual envy, even sometimes anger, inordinate indignation, and dejection of the soul. In this way beginners sometimes abandon the interior life, and give themselves in an immoderate manner either to study out of curiosity, ambition, or external activity in a merely natural manner, that is not Christian, not truly apostolic, nor fruitful.

These defects can be reduced to two, namely, to spiritual sensuality and to spiritual pride, from which follows, sensible consolation having failed, spiritual sloth.

As St. John of the Cross shows (*ibid.*), when beginners actively and generously fight against these defects, they are not rarely *passively purified* by God. This Saint says: "The souls of beginners enter into this dark (passive) night of the senses, when God little by little frees them from the state of beginners where one advances by (discursive) meditation and introduces them into the state of proficients, where contemplation begins. It is necessary to pass through this way so that one may become perfect and arrive at intimate union with God"(*The Dark Night*, bk. 1, c. 1). "The passive purification is common, and happens in many beginners," namely, in those who do not go back, or do not remain as retarded souls. (*Ibid.* bk. 2, c. 8). (Likewise, see bk. II, c. 13, and *The Spiritual Canticle*, before the first stanza; stanzas 4, 6, and 22.)

In *The Dark Night* (bk. 1, c. 9), St. John of the Cross gives *three signs* of this purification of the senses:

First sign: *The soul no longer finds consolation; neither in divine things proposed by way of the senses or the imagination, nor in created things*; and therefore it is in great sensible aridity, so that, namely, it may be purified from all spiritual gluttony or sentimentalism. — This aridity, however, does not come from negligence or spiritual sloth, because consolation is also wanting in created things; on the contrary, the vanity of things of the world are then vividly known, which indicates the *gift of knowledge* according to which the defectibility of secondary causes and the gravity of sin are better understood. Nevertheless this aridity might perhaps arise from melancholy. This doubt, however, is removed by the other signs and also from the fact that often the person about whom it is treated is a sound person.

Second sign: *The soul fears to regress, but it has a true desire for God and perfection.* This is a sign that it does not in fact regress. And melancholy is excluded from this by the fact that with this lively desire for God is a due application to the various obligations both of piety and of one's condition, notwithstanding the sensible aridity which continues in prayer. The soul then does not lessen the time of prayer under the pretext of study or the apostolate. — In the fear of regressing, the influence of the *gift of fear* is apparent, namely, the filial fear, or fear of sin; and in the lively desire for God, the influence of the *gifts of piety* and *fortitude*. In this way the soul perseveres in prayer notwithstanding the great and long aridity of the senses.

Third sign: *Then (discursive) meditation becomes, as it were, impossible, but the soul is inclined to a simple gaze at God in aridity.* "And the reason is," says St. John of the Cross, "because God then begins to communicate Himself no longer by way of the senses through the medium of reasoning, but in a purely spiritual manner, *through the simple act of contemplation.*" In this is apparent the influence of the *gift of knowledge*, by which our indigence is understood: "without me you can do nothing," as well as the *gift of piety* from which arises a filial affection towards God as Father. And if the soul is generous, notwithstanding the long aridity of the senses, it is truly purified from sentimentalism, as from spiritual sloth, and it arrives at a more spiritual knowledge of God and of self, and moreover to a love more prompt for the service of God. In this way the virtue of religion is purified, which attains to a true devotion of the will even when sensible devotion is completely lacking.

During this passive purification of the senses, God often permits *strong temptations against chastity and patience*, that is, against the virtues which are in the sensitive part of the soul, so that there may be meritorious resistance, and a great increase of these virtues; for it does not then suffice to resist slightly, heroic generosity is required; and in this way, through this passive purification of the senses, the inferior part of the soul is fully subordinated to the superior, and it becomes completely docile.

After this passive purification of the senses the soul attains to the state of the proficients or to the *illuminative way,* or "the way of infused contemplation"; St. John of the Cross says: Now this contemplation proceeds from a living faith illuminated by the gifts of understanding and wisdom, thus faith becomes penetrating and savoring. The faithful soul advances in this manner for many years. (*The Dark Night,* bk. 1, chap. 14). But there still remain the *defects of the proficients,* concerning which St. John of the Cross speaks: "There are stains of the old man," he says. "For these proficients still suffer from a *heaviness of mind* (in prayer)... distractions, excessive outpouring in regard to exterior things," (*ibid.* bk. 2, chap. 2) or even a natural severity towards their neighbor which comes forth from egoism. In this way there is lacking perfect justice, the perfect spirit of the faith, of confidence in God, of charity; and many other defects remain, e.g. one's own judgment in the governing of others, or in teaching or in action. The superior part of the soul is not yet fully subject to God, perfect docility to the Holy Ghost is lacking to it and the seven gifts are not exercised as would be necessary, they are still in a certain way bound.

At that time the active and also the passive purification need to be completed, in order that the virtues which are in the upper part of the soul, namely, humility and the three theological virtues, may be purified from all imperfect admixture.

St. John of the Cross says: "It is necessary that the stains of the old man, which remain in the spirit (in the depths of the upper faculties), be removed *through the strong lye of the passive purification of the spirit"* (*ibid.* bk. 2, chap. 2).

If the soul perseveres in generosity, God will complete this purification through the infused light by which *God's sublimity* is much better known quasi experimentally, and by opposition *our misery* is known. This light is the light of the gift of understanding, from which a living faith becomes much more penetrating. In this way is possessed in spiritual aridity, a progressive contemplation of God's sublimity and our misery, which are, says St. Catherine of Siena, like the highest point and lowest point of a circle which is always enlarged. From this arises the experience of the *painful presence of God purifying*.

Thus God especially purifies humility, faith, hope and charity, so that more and more the formal motive of these virtues prevails over every inferior motive. — This must be explained briefly.

Humility is the fundamental virtue for removing the impediment of pride, thus it is compared to an excavation to be made for the construction of a building, and so much the deeper it must be, the more the building is due to be high. Likewise, it is compared to a tree's *root* which ought to be so much the deeper in the earth the more the tree is large. Now from our own reflection our frailty is in some way known, but many illusions remain arising from self-judgment and from secret pride. When God wills to take away these illusions, He manifests our frailty and misery through the light of the gift of knowledge and the gift of understanding, so that all false humility is radically taken away and true humility is purified from all dross. Then the purified soul makes his confession very well, not mechanically, but with perfect penetration without any excuse, and the hard divine castigation having come, it says: "This I certainly merited and still more." Then humility truly bends itself down before God's infinite majesty, as if it were nothing: "my substance is as nothing before Thee" and it desires to be esteemed as nothing.

Faith is purified in the same manner: it is the infused virtue by which we believe the mysteries revealed by God on account of the authority of God revealing. But often our faith rises little above the natural truths of religion, or stops at the formulas, at the text by which the supernatural mysteries are expressed, and not less at the external aspect of the mysteries of the Incarnation, Redemption, and Eucharist; nor does it sufficiently penetrate these, so in like manner when we believe in eternal life or the eternity of punishments. Moreover, as regards the motive, we indeed believe on account of the authority of God revealing, but various quite secondary motives help upon which we rely excessively, e.g. because in our society others also so believe, likewise because the conformity of the mysteries with the natural truths of religion and with our natural aspirations is apparent to us.

Would our faith remain very firm if great temptations were to rise up against it; if at the same time God would manifest the mysteries' profundity to us, e.g. the sublimity of His infinite justice towards the reprobate and the gratuity of eternal predestination, the gratuity of the gift of final perseverance, moreover, if in great aridity of spirit there would be no consolation, and the conformity of the faith with our aspirations would not be experimentally known?

Nevertheless the motive of theological faith would remain, namely, God revealed all these mysteries and they are to be believed on account of His authority as infallibly true. — In this manner the faith of the saints is purified and proved, e.g. when the Apostles saw Jesus handed over, scourged, crowned with thorns, condemned to the death of the Cross, and crucified. Likewise, on Calvary itself the faith of the Blessed Virgin Mary, St. John, and St. Mary Magdalene was tried. Afterwards the holy martyrs suffered amidst prolonged torments; again, many saints in an internal manner underwent strong temptations against the faith, such as Bl. Henry Suso for ten years, and St. Vincent de Paul for four.[1] So very many saints resisted similar temptations by petitioning the actual efficacious grace for overcoming them,

---

1 St. Vincent de Paul had generously accepted a special trial for liberating some professor of theology from great temptations against the faith. And then he was vehemently tempted for four years in the same way. The temptations against the faith were so strong, such that he wrote the Creed on a paper which he placed upon his breast, under his garments. And when the temptations were more vehement, St. Vincent used to press the Creed upon his heart, as a sign of his protestation or profession of faith; then for four years he made heroic acts of this virtue, which in the end was very much strengthened and purified from all imperfection. His faith was in this way made more contemplative, penetrating and savoring, and even amidst the disturbances of this world this saint was thus conserving a great, irradiating interior life, and attained to the rare contemplation of the mystical body of Christ, as he was constantly seeing Jesus in the abandoned children, in the captives, in those detained in prison, and by this divine light his charity was doing immense good.

and in this way they made heroic acts of faith on account of this sole formal motive: God revealed these mysteries, to be believed on account of His authority. At the end of this torment, their faith was perfectly purified, more firm, truly contemplative, no longer stopping at formulas, or at the external aspect of the mysteries, but penetrating them; in this manner the saints lived by faith, so that the supernatural life will have been in the end for them, as it were, the only true life.

Hope also needs a similar purification. It is the infused virtue through which we expect with a firm confidence to obtain eternal life by the divine help. We ought to expect the possession of God on account of His mercy and assisting omnipotence. — In this way we indeed hope, but at the beginning of the spiritual life our infused hope is not sufficiently distinguished from human hope, by which we expect some temporal goods which perhaps might harm us; and although the motive of our hope is God assisting, we have excessive confidence in human helps, of protectors, of friends, in our virtues, in our works, which progress happily enough.

But if God were to take away the expected temporal goods, and at the same time the secondary motives of confidence, the helps of friends, the esteem of Superiors; and if He were to show us our fragility rather than our virtue; if at the same moment temptations against hope were to arise; would our hope remain firm, on account of this sole motive: God does not command impossible things, He does not abandon one crying to Him, He is always the merciful and assisting omnipotent God? So the hope of the saints has been purified, e.g. when the devil was saying to St. Catherine of Siena: "To what avail all your mortifications? If you are predestined, you will be saved without them; and if you are not predestined, even with them you will be damned." St. Catherine replied: "But to what avail your temptations? If I am predestined, these temptations notwithstanding, I will be saved; and if I am not predestined, even without them I will be damned." Then the devil left her. — Sometimes similar temptations rise up in severe suffering, consequently one must pray very much for the suffering by teaching them special prayers for the visitation of the sick and for the commendation of the soul.

Finally, *charity* is purified in the same way. It is the virtue by which we love God on account of Himself, as a friend, by reason of His infinite goodness to be loved above all things; and we love our neighbor on account of God, in order that he may glorify God with us now and in eternity. In this way we indeed love God and our neighbor, but often with notable admixed imperfection coming forth out of self-love, for we also love God on account of the consolation received from Him, and our neighbor on account of the gratitude which he shows to us and the like, and on account of various utilities.

When God wills to lead the soul of one of His children to pure love, He progressively takes away not only all sensible consolation, but also spiritual consolation for many months; and in like manner, He permits indifference and sometimes ingratitude on the part of a beloved neighbor, and it seems that we can do no good. Then God must be loved on account of this true motive, because He is the infinite good in Himself, infinitely better than all His benefits; and in like manner, our neighbor must be loved on account of God, because he is the son of God or can still become a son of God.

In this way the charity of St. Teresa of the Child Jesus was purified at the end of her life from all admixture of self-love. Then the sweetness of God's love is united with the fortitude of a love which perseveres even in spiritual aridity. This leads to the love of the cross in a reparative life for the conversion of sinners according to the example of suffering Christ and His sorrowful mother.

Conclusion: From all these things it is quite evidently established that the virtues are purified proportionally as to their proper object, with their formal motive more and more prominent; in this way the three formal motives of the theological virtues appear as three stars of the first magnitude in the night of the spirit, namely, the first Truth revealing, or the Authority of God revealing; the Mercy and assisting Omnipotence; and the infinite Goodness to be loved above all things.

By this very fact it is evident that this passive purification is necessary for the full purification of the Christian life, as says

St. John of the Cross, and it leads to infused contemplation of the mysteries of the faith and to intimate union with God.

From these propositions it is also evident that in the life of God's servants two particularly obscure periods are generally found, like two *tunnels* (passageways, covered walks), namely, the dark night of the senses and the dark night of the spirit. Sometimes it is historically difficult to say how the souls thus tested in this obscurity have overcome the vehement temptations. But if they have come out from the first night with already sufficiently manifest heroicity of virtues, and if they have come out from the second night with more manifest heroicity, this is a sign that they have not lost the right way in these nights, or that, if at some moment they will have lost it, just as Peter during the Passion when he denied the Lord, Providence lifted them up, so that they might generously continue the ascent until the end. Hence the obscurity of these two periods is not an objection, but on the contrary it is turned into an argument in favor of the heroicity of the soul, for true heroicity is not ascribed except after a fight and victory against great temptations, which especially at these times are raised up by the devil; and the soul does not conquer them unless it pass through these two storms, and acquire proportionate merit. In this way the interior sufferings of God's servants can be illustrated in the causes of beatification, so that it may better appear theologically how these sufferings wonderfully concur towards purification and sanctity, according to the passage of St. Paul: *all things work together unto good, to such as according to his purpose are called to be saints* (Rom. 8:28).

CHAPTER VI

ON MENTAL PRAYER
particularly for the priest

Prayer in general is the "elevation of the mind towards God, by which we ask from Him necessary or convenient things for salvation" (II-II, q. 83, a. 1); and vocal prayer ought to lead to mental prayer, which is like an intimate conversation with God (*Imit.*, 2, c.1).

Mental prayer normally develops with the progress of the interior life. *In the purgative way*, for avoiding sin, many considerations and reflections are required to arrive at firm resolutions, which properly pertain to the *virtue of prudence* under the direction of faith.

Then, when the passions are more regulated, and are, so to speak, asleep, prayer becomes more affective, and then the *virtue of religion* predominates with the *gift of piety*, by considering the four ends of sacrifice: adoration, reparation, petition and thanksgiving.

Finally, with progress, the soul arrives at *contemplative prayer*, which can be called *theological prayer*, as it especially proceeds from the theological virtues with the corresponding gifts of understanding and wisdom. Then the soul "aims chiefly at union with and enjoyment of God" (II-II, q. 24, a. 9).

* * *

1. The method of discursive prayer is described well by St. Francis de Sales (*Introduction to the Devout Life*, part 2, chap. 1 to 10). In it there are three parts:

The first part is the *prayer's preparation*, according as the soul places itself in the presence of God, humbly asks His assistance, and proposes to itself a subject of meditation, e.g. concerning the Lord's Passion; concerning death; concerning the particular judgment after death; concerning hell; concerning purgatory; concerning heaven; concerning our principle duties, the duties of religion and the duties of state to be fulfilled in a Christian manner.

The second is *meditation or considerations* properly so-called about the subject chosen; as for example the Lord's Passion, not only considered under the sensible aspect, but under the spiritual aspect, with the principle practical consequences for us. It is the same about death and about God's judgment. It is the weighing of the thing considered, and then the soul speaks to itself.

The third part contains *affections and resolutions*. That is, the soul not only ought to speak with itself by weighing the object of consideration, but it ought to speak with God by ordering towards Him its desire, its affective and also effective charity, by moving itself more firmly towards mortification of the passions and towards the imitation of Christ. — The resolutions pertain to prudence which directs one's life.

The conclusion of mental prayer is the thanksgiving, and the supplication of grace for keeping the resolutions. In this way, good beginners make discursive prayer, for which many considerations and reflections are required, so that little by little the soul may be elevated above sensible things, and tend more generously towards God. Some make their meditation by slowly reading the Gospel, or the *Imitation of Christ*; others by hearing Mass, by considering its various parts; others by slowly reciting the Rosary, with meditation on the mysteries; others by slowly saying the Lord's Prayer from the whole heart.

* * *

2. Affective prayer. In it considerations are more brief, and the affections predominate under the form of adoration, of thanksgiving, of contrition, and of desire or petition. Hence it is not surprising that St. Julian Eymard insists upon the four ends of sacrifice, which are adoration, thanksgiving, reparation and petition for divine aid. Thus, in this prayer the virtue of religion with the gift of piety is particularly apparent, from which arises a filial affection towards God as the Father. Now the virtue of religion and the gift of piety are in the will, hence it is not surprising that this prayer may be called affective. (Cf. St. Julian

Eymard, *Meditations for Spiritual Exercises at the Feet of Jesus in the Sacrament*, Turin, 1934, vol. 3, p. 82-88.)

Affective prayer, according to the ends of sacrifice, is normally made as follows:

Firstly, when the soul places itself in the presence of God, *adoration* begins, namely, it adores God's infinite excellence and goodness, which is the source of all graces; it also adores Christ's humanity present in the Eucharist and which is immolated in an unbloody manner in the Mass. In this way adoration daily becomes more sublime and more profound, and meanwhile that is verified which St. Thomas says: "Adoration chiefly consists in an interior reverence of God," by practically acknowledging His infinite excellence and by professing ourselves to be nothing of ourselves. (II-II, q. 84, a. 2, ad 2.)

Secondly, there follows *thanksgiving for all God's benefits*, namely, of Creation, of the elevation to the order of grace, of the Incarnation, of the Redemption, for the benefits which we individually receive, even before our birth according as we came into the world in a Christian family, and thereafter until now.

Thirdly, normally *reparation for sins committed* follows: by asking pardon and the grace of a deeper contrition, so that the remains of sin, bad dispositions, particularly the inordinate love of oneself, egoism, the root of the concupiscence of the eyes, of concupiscence of the flesh, of the pride of life, and of the seven capital sins may be taken away from our soul. This is the remedy for self love, which is in the depth of the soul like a bad root impeding the progress of the very good root, namely, charity. And in this reparation, together with the virtue of religion, humility and penitence are exercised.

Fourthly, there finally comes the *petition* of the graces necessary for us individually for persevering until death, and also for saving all souls, as does Jesus Himself, always living to make intercession for us, particularly in the Mass, of which He is the principle Priest.

Now since the virtue of religion is commanded by charity, at the end of this prayer *charity* predominates, affective charity towards God the Father, towards Jesus Christ, "heart to heart";

and not only affective charity, but also the love of conformity with the divine will and zeal or the fervor of charity towards God little loved by men. With this is a lively desire for the extension of His kingdom, and also for the salvation of souls and for the conversion of sinners. For this, the spirit of sacrifice greatly helps, by which this prayer is animated according to the four ends of sacrifice.

As Fr. Maynard, O.P., observes in his *Treatise on the Interior Life,* 1899, 1, 168; and Saudreau, in *The Stages of the Spiritual Life*, 1935, 1, 269; and in the writings of many ancient authors, affective prayer is not distinguished from contemplation, which is distinguished from discursive meditation. Indeed, in affective prayer the discourse or reasoning is very brief, the affection and the fervor of charity predominate; and therein is a certain *contemplation* which can be called *acquired,* when it does not proceed from a special inspiration of the Holy Ghost. —St. Teresa speaks about this prayer in *The Way of Perfection*, chapters 28 and 29; she calls it active recollection: not rarely there are *sensible consolations* in this affective prayer. St. Teresa distinguishes these from the spiritual taste of infused contemplation, by saying: "These sensible consolations begin with some consideration of ours and are ended in God, while the spiritual taste of infused spiritual contemplation descends from God." (*Interior Castle*, the Fourth Mansion, chap. 1). St. John of the Cross speaks likewise in *Living Flame of Love*, strophe 3, verse 3. St. Jane de Chantal speaks likewise.

Moreover, in affective prayer the soul explicitly tends to its own perfection; in infused contemplation it is more united to God, not by thinking of its own perfection, but rather by desiring God's and Christ's glory. Some souls in affective prayer have a very ardent devotion towards the Eucharist, as says Libermann cited by Saudreau in *The Stages of the Spiritual Life*, 1, 275.

At first glance it seems that this fervor indicates mystical prayer, or mystical contemplation, but Fr. Libermann does not believe this, because this fervor is already found in souls which have not yet passed through the aridity of the passive purification of the senses, in which infused contemplation begins, according to St. John of the Cross. — In these souls not yet passively purified, grace works on the surface of the soul, in the sensitive part, but it does not yet penetrate deeper. Hence this fervor is more vehement than solid, firm, and stable; the contrary is verified among the true contemplatives. This is especially apparent in the trials which these persons do not yet bear with generosity, when sensible consolations have been withdrawn.

More slowly, after the long aridity of the senses well endured with faith and confidence, they will be stronger and more constant. Then at the moment of prayer, ordinary grace, less vehement but more intense, will penetrate them more deeply, even to the depth of the soul, by infusing light and love by which they will be more intimately united to God; and then their prayer will be properly contemplative and mystical, as Saudreau notes well in *The Stages of the Spiritual Life*, 1, 277.

Are there some souls which do not advance in prayer, even though they are in the state of grace and they fulfill their strict obligations?

The spiritual authors affirm this, as for example, Saudreau notes: There are souls which only do for God that which is obligatory, and not more, but they neglect mortification, or abnegation; they still love useless readings, strolls simply for pleasure, and other superfluities, such as tobacco, while its price might better be given in the form of alms for the poor. Likewise there are those who desire the esteem of men, who do as they please and also impose their own will; all those who through the lack of abnegation are held back by some attachment and do not have the liberty of spirit in order that they may love God's will in all things. Then during prayer it is not surprising that they remain in the dryness of tepidity and they cannot understand how much mortified souls love intimate prayer, and how much peace and fortitude they find in conversation with God. (*Loc. cit.*, 1, 291.)

* * *

3. Concerning theological prayer, which disposes to infused contemplation. This prayer starts from humility and religion;

afterwards it proceeds from faith, hope and charity, and ends in contemplation, which comes forth from the gifts of understanding and wisdom which are in all just men.

Firstly, this prayer starts *from an act of humility*, which is the fundamental virtue for removing pride. For every prayer ought to be humble, namely, with a consciousness of our neediness. — This act of humility is at the same time *with an act of adoration* of God present in the Eucharist and in the soul of the just. "We have this treasure in clay vessels."

Secondly, this prayer, as an elevation of the mind to God, proceeds *from faith*. This ought to be an act of faith that is simple, profound, continuous, and is as far as possible about the mysteries of Christ's life or the divine perfections. To this end the words of the Gospels and Psalms often suffice; this simple act of faith is already above discourse. The soul says profoundly: *I believe*, e.g. in Christ's real presence in the Eucharist, which presupposes all other mysteries of the Trinity, Incarnation, Redemption, and of eternal life to be attained.

Already in this there is a certain beginning of contemplation, for the soul already, as it were, sees from afar the fountain of living water springing up unto eternal life.

Thirdly, from this act of faith, the *act of hope* proceeds connaturally, for the soul immediately desires the living fountain pointed out by faith: "As the hart panteth after the fountains of water, so my soul panteth after thee, O God" (Ps. 41:2). In other words, the soul trusts God and hopes in God the benefactor, and beseeches His help to arrive at this living fountain. Then it says not only I believe, but I hope, I desire, and I energetically long to attain. — St. Thomas explains this well, saying: "By faith the intellect apprehends those things which we hope for and love. Hence, in the order of generation, faith precedes hope and charity. In like manner, a man loves a thing because he apprehends it as his good. Now from the very fact that a man hopes to be able to obtain some good through someone, he looks on the man in whom he hopes as a good of his own. Hence, for the very reason that a man hopes in someone, he proceeds to love him. So that in order of generation, hope precedes charity as regards their respective acts," but in the order of perfection it is the opposite. (I-II, q. 62, a. 4.)

Fourthly, in this way, therefore, after the act of hope in God the benefactor, the *act of affective charity* connaturally emerges, by which we love the benefactor not only on account of His benefits, but also on account of Himself, because He is infinitely better in Himself than His gifts. Towards the affection of charity, sensibility can concur in an inferior manner; this can be useful, agreeably to the harmony of the faculties, but is not necessary, and this harmony is removed in time of aridity or temptation, in which nevertheless there can be a more intense act of charity. That which is therefore necessary, is a spiritual, supernatural, lofty, deep, tranquil affection, which is much more secure and fruitful than the emotions of sensibility. This act of charity is expressed as follows: e.g. O Lord, grant that I do not lie when I affirm to Thee my love; grant that it may be sincere and true.

This *affective* charity ought to become *effective*, namely, not only by saying: "Lord, I love Thee," but "in all things I *determine* to accomplish Thy will." In this way the resolution is not only general, but also particular about such an inclination to be conquered. — It ought to be observed that the three first petitions of the Lord's Prayer correspond to the three theological virtues: Our Father... hollowed or glorified be Thy name (through faith), Thy kingdom come (this is the object of hope), Thy will be done (namely, through our not only affective but also effective charity).

Finally, in prayer, faith's knowledge and hope's and charity's love are, as it were, united, *under the inspiration of the gift of wisdom, in a simple and affectionate look at the divine goodness.* In this manner, infused contemplation begins. Just as a painter contemplates the sensible nature, just as a child contemplates or affectionately looks at the countenance of his mother, so the Christian soul in prayer contemplates God according to the passage of the Psalmist: "O taste, and see that the Lord is sweet." In this way the just soul arrives at a quasi-experimental knowledge of God. It does not have an immediate experience of God Himself, but it knows God, as it were, experimentally through the filial affection which the special inspiration of the

Holy Ghost stirs up in us, according to that passage: "The Spirit himself giveth testimony to our spirit that we are the sons of God" (Rom. 8:16). St. Thomas says in his Commentary: He gives this testimony "through the filial affection" which He stirs up in us through a special inspiration, i.e. "an infused act of charity," and with a certain moral certitude we distinguish this filial affection from the more or less similar natural act, in which would be sentimentalism, without sufficient conformity to the divine will.

This mental prayer so ordained is an elevation of the mind to God, proceeding initially from humility and from religion, afterwards from the three theological virtues, and finally, more or less hiddenly, from the gifts of wisdom and of understanding.

Hence, in it, knowledge and love are more and more united in the affective knowledge of God inspired by the Holy Ghost. In this way it is like the *breathing of the soul* which breathes in truth and grace and breathes out love. It is a sort of protracted spiritual communion for a half an hour. And little by little discursive prayer and then affective prayer disposes to it, just as it itself disposes to higher contemplation, in passive recollection and in the passive prayer of the quiet about which speaks St. Teresa in the fourth Mansion (*Interior Castle*).

This theological prayer reconciles the simplicity of the ancient authors with the sometimes exceedingly complicated method of the moderns. And it can be applied to the various subjects to be considered, particularly to the consideration of the petitions of the Lord's Prayer, as is explained by St. Teresa in *The Way of Perfection*, chap. 30 ff.

In this way are better understood the three stages of prayer about which St. Thomas speaks in II-II, q. 180, a. 6, where it is discussed: firstly, about the straight movement; secondly, about the oblique movement in the form of a spiral; and thirdly, about the circular movement.

The *straight movement* (B-A) ascends from sensible things to God, and it considers God in the mirror of sensible things, e.g. of nature or parables.

The *oblique* movement (C) in the form of a spiral, ascends just as the winding road of a mountain, e.g. through the joyful, sorrowful, and glorious mysteries of the Most Holy Rosary to the contemplation of God, considered in the mirror of intelligible truths

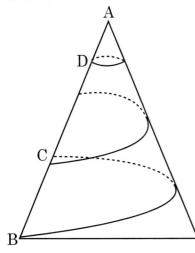

The *circular movement* (D), similar to the flight of an eagle or of a swallow in the highest part of the sky, does not strictly have either a beginning or an end, in this way it differs from reasoning; it is a simple look at the divine goodness, whose irradiation is considered just as the eagle flying circularly considers the irradiation of the sun.

Good prayer, little by little, transforms the character and renders the soul similar to Christ, and it understands His words: "Learn of me because I am meek and humble of heart, and you shall find rest to your souls."

CHAPTER VII

ON EUCHARISTIC WORSHIP
AND ON PRIESTLY PERFECTION
(according to St. Peter Julian Eymard)

On Eucharistic Worship and on the interior life.

It is commonly said, in regard to all Christians, that the Eucharist nourishes the interior life, because it is the nourishment of faith, hope, charity, religion, and the other virtues.

Firstly, for truly it is the *nourishment of faith*, insofar as the Eucharist is like a garland of the mysteries of the faith, as it presupposes the mystery of the redemptive Incarnation of the Son of God, consequently the mystery of the Trinity, the mystery of the elevation of the human race to the life of grace, and it is a pledge of eternal life. In this way only one Eucharistic miracle confirming the truth of the Eucharist, confirms for that reason all the other presupposed mysteries.

Secondly, the Eucharist *nourishes hope*, because hope relies upon the divine help of grace. Now the Eucharist contains not only grace but also the Author of grace, so it is the highest of all the sacraments.

Thirdly, the Eucharist *nourishes charity*, as Communion joins us to Christ and increases especially charity towards God and also towards one's neighbor, a not only affective but also effective charity. In this way the Eucharist is the *bond of charity* uniting the various members of any Christian family without distinction, uniting the poor with the rich, the wise and the ignorant at the same holy table; uniting the peoples of the whole Christianity. In this way two principles are verified: The good is essentially diffusive of itself, and the higher it is, the more full and abundant is the diffusion of itself. While material goods cannot be possessed at the same time and fully by many, spiritual goods not only can be possessed at the same time and fully by many, but what is more, in that case they are possessed by every single one, and if one were to want to exclude others, he would lose charity and simultaneously the possession of the spiritual good. In this way we can all possess at the same time the same truth, the same virtue, the same Christ present after the manner of a substance in the Eucharist, and the same God present obscurely in our souls, and clearly in heaven.

Fourthly, the Eucharist *nourishes religion*, because the highest act of religion is sacrifice, in other words, an act simultaneously internal, external and public. Now the Eucharistic sacrifice is like a sacramental continuation of the sacrifice of the Cross and of infinite value; because the principal priest, that is to say Christ, cannot be more united to God, nor more holy, nor more united with the victim, because He offers Himself, and both the victim and the principal one offering are of infinite value.

On the Eucharistic worship and on the priestly perfection, according to St. Peter Julian Eymard, *Meditations*, vol. 3. — Summary:

I. *On the priesthood and on the spirit of Christ* (p. 186), particularly on the spirit of sacrifice (p.43).

II. *On Eucharistic worship*, on Eucharistic service, and on the priestly perfection; *on the four ends of sacrifice* (80, 82, 83, 85, 87, 206, 159, 161); on the interior life of Jesus in the Eucharist as an example of the principal virtues, charity, religion, humility, and poverty (88, 98, 164); on Eucharistic faith (108-112); on confidence; on charity (103); on reparative charity according to the example of Christ the victim (105); the Litany of the Eucharistic Heart.

III. *Conclusion: On the Eucharist and on priestly perfection* (161); on the Eucharistic vocation (80, 230, 232).

I. — On the priesthood and on the spirit of Christ.

The priest ought to offer the unbloody sacrifice of infinite value; to absolve the penitents, so, as it were, to beget them to the life of grace and to guide them to eternal life; and particularly he ought to evangelize the poor. For this purpose he ought to possess purity, humility, kindness, fruitful charity, for the glory of God and of Christ and the salvation of souls. He ought to follow the example of the Apostles when they instituted the deacons for the ministry of the works of mercy, saying: "But we will give ourselves continually to prayer and to the ministry of the word" (Acts 6:4). Otherwise there is much external labor without fruit: "Having suffered a great deal, but outside the right way." — Moreover the priest ought to say as John the Baptist: "*He must increase: but I must decrease.*"

To this end he ought to live from the spirit of Christ: "He who is joined to the Lord is one spirit with him" (1 Cor. 6:17); "If any man have not the Spirit of Christ, he is none of his" (Rom. 8:9). Now this spirit is the *spirit of truth*: "For this came I into the world; that I should give testimony to the truth" (Jn. 18:37); "You are the light of the world" (Mt. 5:14); "You shall be witnesses unto me" (Acts 1:8). — This spirit is the *spirit of love,* which manifests itself through kindness (Learn of me, because I am meek, and humble of heart: Mt. 11:29) and through zeal even unto death (Christ loved me and delivered himself for me: Gal. 2:20). — Consequently this spirit is the *spirit of sacrifice*: "He that loveth father and mother more than me, is not worthy of me"; "He that taketh not up his cross, and followeth me, is not worthy of me." But this sacrifice yields a hundredfold: "To him that overcometh I will give the hidden manna" (Apoc. 2:17).

II. On Eucharistic worship and on priestly perfection.

This worship of latria is exercised through the worthy celebration of the sacrifice of the Mass, which every day ought to be celebrated with greater faith, hope, charity, and substantial, if not sensible, devotion. It is exercised through Eucharistic Communion and also through visits to the Most Blessed Sacrament, through reparative adoration, supplication and thanksgiving.

Hence there cannot be on earth, greater, more holy, more liturgical worship, in which are exercised the virtues of faith towards Christ hidden under the species, of hope, of charity, of religion, of humility, and the corresponding gifts of the Holy Ghost, from all which things priestly perfection is constituted.

And all, even the weak, the imperfect, can and ought *to aspire* to this perfection, so that they may become true adorers of Christ present in the Eucharist. For arriving at a distinguished state in civil society, great labor is required, as for example, that someone be a lawyer, a doctor, a professor, a jurist, etc., while the most modest priests and simple faithful can come to the Eucharistic worship and if they are truly humble and pious, they can profit much in it, according to the saying of the Lord: "Come to me all you that labor and are burdened, and I will refresh you." For Communion nourishes the soul so that it may be able to avoid sin, resist the temptations of the flesh and of the devil, and so that it may be able to progressively love God "with the whole heart and with the whole soul, with all one's powers and with one's whole mind." — In this way with the progress of charity through Communion and adoration, the seven gifts and docility to the Holy Ghost are also increased.

But especially in this Eucharistic worship two things ought to be considered: firstly, the four ends of the sacrifice ought to be considered; and secondly, the virtues of which Jesus gives us an example in the Eucharist itself.

* * *

1. The four ends of the sacrifice ought to be considered attentively.

The first end of sacrifice is *adoration*. In this way the holocaust ordained to adoration is the principal sacrifice. And men often forget the adoration of God. They adore the flesh, riches, the progress of science, or reason, themselves, and in this way is had society-worship, government-worship, and rationalism, which is the worship of reason above all things, etc. And often Christ the Savior is abandoned, not only by unbelieving and indifferent men, but also by ungrateful faithful, even sometimes by his ministers, who seem to love Him as mercenaries on account of some reward, and not as sons; they seem to love Him not on account of Himself, but on account of themselves. In this way adoration commanded by charity is lacking, because there is little charity.

Often in certain parishes, Christ present in the Eucharist remains alone for nearly the entire week, while He would be able to daily be a fountain of grace, because among the faithful not even one comes to Mass except on Sunday, and never for the sake of visitation of the Most Blessed Sacrament. In this is seen not only little charity, but also little faith and hope, which are normally shown through the virtue of religion which they command.

Hence, *adoration* of Christ the Savior, present in the Eucharist, is to be greatly commended; this adoration of itself repairs many instances of ingratitude, great indifference and negligence of salvation.

The second end of Eucharistic **sacrifice** is *thanksgiving* for all the divine benefits, namely, for Creation and the elevation of the human race to the order of grace and glory, for the redemptive Incarnation, for the very institution of the Eucharist and of all the graces proceeding from it, for the innumerable Masses and Communions accomplished during twenty centuries for the purpose of the strengthening of souls.

Many men, by never thinking about these benefits, are ungrateful in the highest degree, and the ingratitude is so much the greater the more the benefit was precious and universal. Children generally exhibit some gratitude to their parents, but many men show none to God who is the source of all goods.

Since, however, this ingratitude is not only individual but also collective; the thanksgiving ought to be collective and public. This is the second end of the Eucharist, whence its name is chosen. In fact, the Eucharist commemorates among us all God's very lofty benefits which it presupposes, namely, the Incarnation and Redemption, and it continually applies to us the fruits of the Redemption. Hence, as St. John Fisher, the English martyr, used to say, the Mass is like a spiritual sun which enlightens and warms us daily; this he was saying to the Lutherans of his time who were denying the Mass, and whose temples were remaining cold, without the heat of the spiritual sun. These fresh benefits of the Mass and Communion call for a new thanksgiving. The worship towards the Eucharistic Heart of Jesus is essentially ordained to this thanksgiving for the institution of the Eucharist. This institution, as is evident, calls for a special thanksgiving. The expression 'Eucharistic Heart of Jesus' especially signifies the Heart of Jesus which gave to us the Eucharist and gives it again daily.

The third end of sacrifice is *reparation,* on account of the sins committed against God, and in particular sacrileges, sometimes the most perverse, accomplished under the inspiration of the devil; only God knows the enormity of certain sacrileges, which call to mind the betrayal of Judas. For the sake of repairing these abominations, the Mass is to be holily celebrated, and the Eucharist publicly exposed is to be adored.

In this way, the accidental glory is restored to God and to Christ, which is denied to them through the aforesaid sins. This reparation gives to Christ the accidental joy which many deny to Him. This reparation calls to mind that which holy Veronica did during the Passion when she wiped the brow of the Lord with a cloth, on which remained Christ's likeness.

In this manner, public reparation blocks God's great castigations, equally public, which the world deserves for its iniquities. And at the same time, mercy is besought for sinners in order that they return to the way of salvation and to penance. Among the souls which perfectly comprehend this end of sacrifice, certain ones offer themselves as victims; they are in the world as "lightning rods," for averting God's terrible castigations. It is said in the Canticle of Tobias, 13:5: "He hath chastised us for our iniquities: and he will save us for his own mercy." The reparation in Eucharistic worship obtains this mercy. In this worship the reparation offered in the sacrifice of the Cross continues.

The fourth end of sacrifice is *supplication* for impetrating the divine aid, and all the graces necessary for salvation, particularly the grace of final perseverance, which is not an object of merit, but can be obtained through the impetrative power of prayer, and especially of the greatest prayer, which is contained in the very oblation of the sacrifice of the Mass, in which continues "the intercession of Christ always living to intercede for us." And we ought to unite to His intercession, just as to His adoration, reparation and thanksgiving, in such a way that the value of our actions may be greatly increased.

This intercession of Christ always continues in the Eucharist even while the celebration of the Mass ceases. And thus we ought to unite ourselves to the prayer of the Savior, not only by praying for ourselves individually, but also for the Church; for the pastors that they may receive zeal and fortitude from God; for peace; for the concord of nations; and for the liberty of the Church and the sanctification of souls. Likewise we ought to unite to His prayer for the conversion of unbelievers and sinners.

Among the souls which understand well this end of sacrifice, certain ones are more contemplative, just as Mary Magdalene at the feet of the Savior, or just as an Angel is an adorer of the heavenly King. Or better: they are compared to the image of the Blessed Virgin Mary in the cenacle after the Lord's Ascension, and they, as it were, continue her prayer of supplication for the Church.

This fourfold consideration of the ends of sacrifice is very practical, because the soul, firstly, by adoring, gazes upon God *in eternity*; then it gazes upon *the past with respect to the benefits received*, by giving thanks; *the past with respect to the sins forgiven*; and finally *the future* by entreating the divine assistance.

At the same time this Eucharistic worship so conceived, intimately unites us with Christ the priest, with His intimate reparative adoration, with His intercession and thanksgiving.

* * *

2. *In the next place the interior life of Jesus Christ in the Eucharist must be more loftily considered insofar as He is an example to us of the principal virtues.*

To treat theologically about this point, it must be observed that Christ present in the Eucharist is Christ glorious in heaven; in other words, He is no longer a wayfarer, He does not suffer, nor does He merit, but He exercises *the virtues* according as they remain in heaven, e.g. by adoring, by interceding, by giving thanks, etc. Moreover, Christ in heaven knows that which happens on earth, and consequently He knows of the Eucharistic worship which increases His accidental beatitude, and by opposition, the profanations which deny Him this accidental beatitude.

Hence about this it ought to be observed with St. Thomas that in heaven neither faith nor hope remain, but in place of faith there is the beatific vision, in place of hope the lasting possession of God, nevertheless charity, the moral virtues, and the seven gifts remain. That is to say: The moral virtues remain as to that which is *formal*, namely, the holy disposition, but not as to that which is *material*: "There will be no concupiscences and pleasure in matters of food and sex; nor fear and daring about dangers of death, nor distributions and exchanges of things employed in this present life" (I-II, q. 67, a. 1).

These things having been set forth, it is easy to understand that which St. Peter Eymard says (p. 88), by distinguishing that which is said in the proper sense and that which is said metaphorically. It is also true to say in the proper sense: In the Eucharist Jesus no longer has an external life, He no longer visits the sick, preaches and the like. He remains in the tabernacle "like a prisoner of love," or in other words, voluntarily. He does not exercise the external senses with respect to those things which surround the Eucharist; but He knows all these things in a higher manner in heaven through infused knowledge and the beatific vision. Hence, Christ in the Eucharist has only an interior and most perfect life; in this way He teaches us solitude, silence, and recollection. Christ wishes to give us an example of many virtues, namely, of *charity* towards His Father and towards souls; of *religion*, as He always adores, gives thanks and intercedes; of *humility* and of *obedience* in compliance with perfect subjection to the divine will; of *kindness*, for never was an inordinate passion in Him.

Especially, as St. Peter Julian Eymard says: The interior life of Jesus in the Eucharist is a *life of love* towards His Father, to Whom He always offers his actions, His sacramental state, and His past Passion, commemorated in the Mass. Likewise, His life is a life of love towards men to be saved. His Heart is the center of all hearts (p.90).

The Blessed Virgin Mary excellently possessed this Eucharistic devotion, "Her heart was drawn to the divine Tabernacle like iron to the magnet" (p. 93). And just as some saints had the miraculous privilege of conserving in themselves the sacramental species without corruption until the following communion, so this privilege ought not to be denied to the Blessed Virgin Mary.

In light of these principles of St. Peter Julian Eymard, it is deservedly spoken about Eucharistic humility, about Eucharistic poverty, about Eucharistic faith and about Eucharistic charity; e.g. he says: In the Eucharist, Christ's divinity, glory and power are hidden; likewise His humanity, Jesus *is in a most humble* (poor[1]) *state*; He continually works for the sanctification of souls but in silence, in a mysterious manner, so that men see nothing. In this way, the soul which is intimately united with Christ present in the Eucharist has an intense interior life of love, but exteriorly remains as a poor man, a servant and a lowly man.[2] He sometimes exults interiorly, but he does not show it exteriorly: "his life is hidden with Christ in God."

This passage is very beautiful: "The virtues of her soul should be sublime and perfect, but their manner of expression, simple and ordinary. In a word, their perfection must be like live coals beneath the ashes" (p. 95). In this manner, Christ's Heart is an ardent furnace of charity hidden under the sacramental species (completely the opposite of theater).

With humility, Christ in the Eucharist exercises *charity*, and His charity is sweet, patient, and generous. He is sweet particularly with the poor, with the afflicted. He is patient in waiting for us. He is generous in regard to all; He precedes them,

---

1 *pavero*

2 *pauper, servus et humilis.* Cf. "Panis Angelicus," from hymn of Matins of Corpus Christi (*Translator's note*).

even His enemies, and attracts them to conversion. Nay, rather, in the Eucharist Jesus remains as a *victim of love*, immolated in an unbloody manner in the Mass; in this way He attracts many truly faithful souls to a reparative life.

All these things are very well expressed in the litany of the Eucharistic Heart of Jesus, which contains an ascending climax, from the state of humiliation in which the Savior is in the Eucharist, to the lofty and intimate union to which He calls generous souls.[3]

---

3 This very beautiful prayer is particularly appropriate for adoration of the Most Blessed Sacrament.

PRAYER
TO THE EUCHARISTIC HEART OF JESUS

Eucharistic Heart of Jesus, sweet companion of our exile,
    I adore Thee,
Eucharistic Heart of Jesus,
Lonely Heart, Humiliated Heart, Forsaken Heart,
Forgotten Heart, Despised Heart, Outraged Heart,
Heart disowned by men,
Heart which loves our hearts,
Heart begging to be loved,
Heart patient in waiting for us,
Heart thoughtful in answering our prayers,
Heart eager to be entreated,
Heart perennial source of new graces,
Silent Heart, desirous to speak to souls,
Heart, sweet refuge of the hidden life,
Heart, master of the secrets of the divine union,
Heart of Him who sleeps yet always watches,
Eucharistic Heart of Jesus, have mercy on us,
Jesus Host, I want to console Thee,
I unite myself to Thee, I immolate myself with Thee,
I annihilate myself before Thee,
I want to forget myself in order to think only of Thee,
I desire to be forgotten and despised for Thee,
I desire to be understood and loved only by Thee,
I will be silent to listen to Thee, and I will let go of myself to disappear
in Thee,
        Give me the grace to quench Thy thirst for my salvation; Thy ardent thirst for my sanctity; and that, being purified, I may render Thee a pure and true love.

* * *

III. — **Conclusion:** *Eucharistic worship so conceived effectively leads to priestly perfection* (p. 161, 80, 230, 232).

This is because the actual, efficacious graces which perfect the soul are derived from Christ really present in the Eucharist, just as when Christ, after His resurrection, says to Peter, so that he may repair his denial, "Simon, son of John, lovest thou me? He saith to him: yea, Lord, thou knowest that I love thee" (Jn. 21:16). Then Christ says to him: "Feed my lambs and sheep," and He foretells to him his martyrdom. This prediction is simultaneous with the grace which already prepares Peter for the constancy of a martyr. And there is a similar influence of Christ present in the Eucharist, but in a hidden manner; it is an influence inspiring an efficacious and persevering love.

In this, faith is often tried, just as when St. Peter Julian Eymard was waiting for vocations; they were not coming, nay, his only son went away; when Peter Julian Eymard saw this, he remained before the Most Blessed Sacrament, saying: "Lord, I will remain here kneeling until my son returns." And after three or four hours he returned, and thereafter many and very good vocations came, so that his Congregation bore very abundant fruits not only in France, Italy, and in other regions of Europe, but also in North and South America. Through this trial of faith the soul is led to perfection.

I do not want anymore to prolong Thy waiting: Take me, I devote myself to Thee.

I give Thee all my deeds, my whole spirit to be enlightened by Thee, my heart to be led by Thee, my will to be fixed to Thee, my misery to be assisted by Thee, my soul and my body to be fed by Thee.

Eucharistic Heart of Jesus, whose blood is the life of my soul, may I no longer live, but rather may Thou alone live in me.

Amen.

(An indulgence of 200 days; Leo XIII, February 6, 1899.)

Who exactly are called to sanctity through this life (p. 230)?

There are those who have accepted a Eucharistic vocation. Jesus says: "No man can come to me, except the Father, who hath sent me, draw him" (Jn. 6:44). Now the Father draws all men to salvation, but not always in the same manner. All Christians are indeed called to Eucharistic worship, and in a higher degree priests are called, but among them some are specially attracted.

What is a Eucharistic vocation, according to St. Peter Julian Eymard (p. 230)?

It is a *special attraction of grace*, at the same time sweet and strong, as if the Lord were to say: "Come to my sanctuary." This attraction, little by little, becomes *dominant*, if there is no resistance.

Then, if the soul is faithful and responds to this attraction, it finds *peace,* as if it had found its natural and fitting place and its spiritual food: "I have found the place of my repose." Books and spiritual discourses do not help enough, a more profound prayer before the Most Blessed Sacrament is required.

Finally, this attraction of grace guides the soul so that it completely offers itself *to the service of the Eucharist*, so that it may become a *true adorer of Jesus Christ* present in the Sacrament. That is, not only so that it may be saved; that it acquire virtues; nor only that it save other souls, because God and Christ are to be loved more than one's neighbor; but also so that it may respond to that invitation of the Savior: "The true adorers shall adore the Father in spirit and in truth. For the Father also seeketh such to adore him" (Jn. 4:23).

In adoration conceived in this way, is included that which St. Thomas with the ancient authors called contemplation of divine things, for this contemplation proceeds from a living faith enlightened by the gifts of the Holy Ghost, and commands the virtue of religion, of which the highest act is sacrifice, especially the sacrifice of adoration.

Eucharistic worship thus profoundly conceived leads to true priestly perfection, by which the priest, under the perpetual influence of Christ present in the Eucharist, becomes *another Christ.*

Many through this way have in fact reached sanctity. We therefore ought to humbly and confidently aspire to it, daily beseeching the efficacious grace to this end, for the glory of God and of the salvation of souls.

Lightning Source UK Ltd.
Milton Keynes UK
UKOW04f0321091213

222608UK00001B/89/P